GREAT

A **PocketScroll**® Book

IDEAS

Practical suggestions for parenting,
teaching and personal growth

AVI SHULMAN

P'TACH OF PHILADELPHIA

is an organization which has existed for over twenty three years. As part of a national Jewish organization which provides services to children with learning disabilities, we in the Greater Philadelphia area, have expanded our services to assist children with a wide range of learning difficulties.

We have sponsored Hebrew resource room services in area day schools and high schools, provided individualized instruction to children who need help to maintain themselves in these schools, and offered a referral system that links children with appropriate tutors and therapists.

In addition, we have employed educational consultants to provide staff training so that we can better meet the individual needs of our students.

It is clear to us that these children can succeed when they are perceived as children who have gifts, not deficits, and supports are given to them to realize their full potential.

With your financial support, P'TACH can provide resources so that children with all types of abilities can work together to build a better Jewish world for us all.

P'TACH
Parents for **T**orah for **A**ll **C**hildren

In Memory
of my parents

Rose and Morris Caskey, ע׳ה

Dr. Herbert Caskey

In Memory of
My Beloved Father
Saul Goldman, זצ"ל

Dr. Warren Goldman

In Memory of
Rabbi Herman J. and Edith
Zwillenberg, ז׳ל
and Irving Fenner, ז׳ל

The Zwillenberg Family

In Memory of
Saba and Harry Hollander ז"ל
whose love for children
knew no bounds

Bracha and Ephraim Goldfein

IN HONOR OF

OUR DEAR FRIENDS

THE GLOBMANS

With love from
The Spitzer/Wachs Family

In honor of Khana
🌹 Globman 🌹
and the wonderful work
you do for P'TACH

Thank you very much
The Raikin Family

Best Wishes

The Twersky Family

Dedicated to the P'TACH children by:
SPONSORS

Henchy and David Abraham
Yaela and Neil Baine
Beverly and Toby Bernstein
Harriet and Larry Bernstein
Rabbi & Mrs. Yechiel Biberfeld
Marilyn and Philip Borck and family
Ellen and Michael Braffman
Dr. and Mrs. David Chase
Elise and Marty Ciner
Congregation Beth Solomon
Dr. and Mrs. Sol Daiches
Ephraim and Lisa Dardashti
Gary and Andrea Diamond
In memory of Sylvia Eichler, ע"ה
    by Linda and Barry Eichler
Daniel & Janet Eisenberg
Cheryl and David Epstein
Miriam Esris
Mr. And Mrs. Michael Feinberg
Drs. Gary and Ruth Feldman
Richie and Janis Fine
Dr. & Mrs. Victor Fishman
Sherman and Susan Frager
Debbi and Marc Frankel
Galena Family
Linda and Norman Garfield
Dr. and Mrs. Leonard Ginsburg
Shimi and Devorah Globman
Yaakov Globman
Adena and Dov Goldman

Brian and Joy Goldstein in memory of
    Sara and Aron Wygoda, ז'ל
Hal and Sue Gordon
Rabbi and Mrs. Fischel Gorin
Bram and Carol Greenberg
Marc and Cindy Henzel
Rosalyn and Irvin Hirsch
Azriel and Rifka Hirschfield
In memory of Ephraim Hoenlein, זצ'ל
    By Erna Hoenlein
Yonina and Zev Jacobson
Larry and Michelle Jonas
Rabbi & Mrs. Eliezer Katz
Mark and Monica Kohn
Stanley and Carole Kops
Talia and David Lebor
Rabbi and Mrs. Abraham Levene
Rabbi & Mrs. Joshua Levy
Dr. E. Robert Libby
Steven and Suzanne Lindell
Lester and Lisa Lipschutz
Bill McCaulley
Ziesel Meth
Mark and Marlene Moster
Erwin and Rochelle Nosenchuk
Phyllis and Charles Parker
Stuart and Pia Pollack

Joel and Judy Pomerantz
Vera Revesz
Jay and Mindy Rosenblum
Allen and Barbara Rothenberg
Dr. and Mrs. Jonathan Schiffman
Albert and Clara Schild
Meir and Linda Seidenwar
David and Kineret Shakow
Harvey and Barbara Sicherman
Barry and Eileen Stieglitz

Avi and Bracha Strimber
In memory of Sol Sved, ז׳ל
    by Betty Sved
Ira and Naomi Sved
Stanley and Jillyan Sved
Dr. and Mrs. Harvey Tannenbaum
Drs. Ronald & Marguerite Werrin
Leon and Tova Wertheimer
Ezra and Susie Wohlgelerenter
Young Israel of the Main Line

לזכר נשמת
In loving memory of our parents
Morris and Ruth Ellis ז׳ל
and
Arthur and Laura Elsner ז׳ל

Nachman and Avigayil Elsner

In Memory of our beloved

parents

Dr. Maurice and Ida Sand ז'ל

Herman and Sadie Rech ז'ל

Rhoda and Stephen Sand

IN LOVING MEMORY OF
Rabbi and Mrs. Minkoff ע"ה
and
Mr. Albert Pransky ע"ה

Bob and Judy Pransky

In Loving Memory of

Chesna Coren, ז'ל   Herman Coren, ז'ל

Marvin Denenberg, ז'ל   Dolores Coren, ז'ל

Bell Gilda, ז'ל

NOT JUST CANDY – Shmuel and Rebecca Dear

Friends of P'TACH

Jack and Alisha Abboudi
Abe and Gail Barnett
Avi and Leah Barr
Harriet and Larry Bernstein
Mr. & Mrs. Bruce Blady
Hansi Bodenheim
Dr. Lance and Dale Dunoff
The Eckmann Family
Larry and Elisa Ellis and family
Len and Gilya Freedman
Dovid & Meira Friedman & Family
In memory of Manny & Yetta Herscher ע'ה
    by Sandy Falcone
Barry and Miriam Gesserman
Mr. & Mrs. David Goodstein
Rabbi Dr. & Mrs. Yakov Gorin
David and Leah Gotlib
Alan and Beth Gottfried
In memory of Edith Gross ע'ה
    by Amy Gross
Nancy and Joel Horwitz
Mr. & Mrs. Levi Keil
Mr. & Mrs. David Klein
Sandy and Michael Kornhauser
Reuvein and Miriam Kovacs
Dr. & Mrs. Mel Lerner and Family
Jonathan and Nomi Levene

Rabbi & Mrs. Boruch Lichtenstein
Rabbi Mordechai Liebling & Lynn Eiser
Mark and Rachel Meles
Jules and Arlene Milgrim
Mr. and Mrs. Robert Moroz
Audrey Whitman and Paul Newman
Dr. Emilie S. Passow
Rakhmiel and Hannah Peltz
Dr. & Mrs. David Popper
Mr. & Mrs. Max Reiser
Douglas R. Reich
Theodore and Tybie Resnik
Roselee and Phil Redelheim
Eva Rosenstock
Rabbi & Mrs. Abraham Shemtov
Albert and Eileen Singer
Mira and Aron Singer
Mr. and Mrs. Jonas Singer
Leonard and Rita Small
Howard and Cathy Snyder
Rabbi and Mrs. Mordechai Terebelo
Rabbi & Mrs. Dovid Wachs
David and Ellen Weiss
Yitzchok and Laya Weinberger
Marc and Mona Yudkoff
Rabbi and Mrs. Yoel Dovid Zeffren
Wertheimer Monuments

חֲנוֹךְ לַנַּעַר עַל פִּי דַרְכּוֹ
גַּם כִּי יַזְקִין לֹא יָסוּר מִמֶּנָּה (משלי כב:ו)

Teach a child according to his way;
when he is old he will not depart from it (Proverbs 22:6)

For copies of this book, information, or interest in future sponsorship
participation, contact:
P'TACH, P.O. Box 310, Wynnewood & Argyle Roads, Ardmore, PA 19003
or phone **(215) 477-7123**

TABLE OF CONTENTS

This book is lovingly dedicated to the memory of

DR. JOSEPH KAMINETSKY z"l

who was National Director of Torah Umesorah for nearly forty years and who built Torah Umesorah into the driving force of Day School/Yeshiva education serving the United States and Canada.

Your life was a special gift to us! You taught us how one person can make a great difference in Klal Yisrael, you taught us how to overcome trials and tribulations, you taught us the meaning of Mokir D'Rabbonim (respect and adherence to gedolim), and you taught us practical emunah in Hashem.

In the name of my family, and the many people whom you have inspired, I thank you for giving us the privilege of sharing in your dream.

DR. KAMINETSKY z"l

r. Joseph Kaminetsky and the story of Torah Umesorah need no introduction to the thousands of families who were involved with the Yeshiva/Day School revolution that took place in the '40's, '50's, '60's, and '70's. But for the generation who came to find "the table set and the food tastefully prepared," the story of Dr. Kaminetsky, his mentors, and his activities, hopes, and dreams is vitally important.

Those of us who had the privilege of working with him were constantly impressed by his indomitable spirit. The hardship of three-weeks-across-the-country bus and train trips, nights on the couch, missed meals, and forgotten promises were all swept away by the excitement of the opening of a new school. The ability to stay focused on a simple, clearly defined objective for over four decades is in itself remarkable. What makes Dr. Kaminetsky's achievements even more remarkable is that the network of Torah Umesorah schools was built in spite of untold frustrations, heartaches, and disappointments which would have deflected a lesser man.

Dr. Kaminetsky was given his mandate by Rav Shraga Feivel Mendlowitz *zt"l* and never allowed any difficulty to turn him aside from fulfilling this mandate. He was truly the trustworthy messenger who always delivered the message. Traveling the country today and finding vibrant Yeshiva Day Schools in many large and small communities, it is hard to imagine the frustration of the early years when "no one would listen."

The concept of an all-day school that teaches Torah was so foreign to the Jews in these communities that, for the most part, they simply ignored the call. The mood of the Jewish community after the Second World War was shock and disbelief about what had happened in Europe, and the determination to maintain the existing Jewish structures — synagogues, Talmud Torahs, Federation, etc. In this mood of doom and gloom, the dream of building a Jewish educational system was beyond the realm of possibility, even for the most optimistic and visionary lay person. But because everyone on Dr. Kaminetsky's staff had the vision — it was possible! Dr. Kaminetsky and his small, loyal staff — Rabbis Bernard

Goldenberg, Lou Nulman, Shea Fishman, Zvi Shurin, Yaakov Fruchter, Dov Lesser, Dov Oustatcher, Moshe Friedman, Alfred Schnell, Mrs. Bernice Brand, and others — had to "sell" the concept of teaching Torah and to create an entire support system: Rabbinical Administrative Board, lay leadership, school organization, enrollment personnel, teacher-training personnel, summer seminars, teacher placement, publications, Olomeinu, *kollelim*, the Fryer Foundation, S.E.E.D., the Parent-Teacher Association, *The Jewish Parent Magazine*, Administrators Association, National Conference of Yeshiva Principals, and other educational services. Not only did they have to create these units, they had to continually raise the funds to make them thrive.

Of all the thousands of images and vignettes that come to my mind of Dr. Kaminetsky — speaking at conventions, conferences, Aish Dos, school visitations, staff meetings, and late-night discussions with principals and lay leaders — the one that I remember best is the *shalosh seudos* at a small convention, when Dr. Kaminetsky was leading everyone in singing and dancing: נצח ישראל לא ישקר, "The Eternity of *Klal Yisrael* will never be falsified."

GREAT IDEAS

by

AVI SHULMAN

his is a unique book ... seventy-one different and often unrelated chapters ... each providing about 10 minutes of stimulating and rewarding reading ... each starting you off on your own thought, on a positive course of immediately useful ideas ... so that you may build your life as you want it.

The purpose of this book is to stimulate constructive thoughts, to give your thoughts improved direction and greater substance, and to provide the kind of motivational thinking which will enable you to deal successfully with yourself, people, and problems.

ABOUT THE AUTHOR

Mr. Avi Shulman was a classroom teacher for over twenty-five years, National Director of Torah Umesorah's S.E.E.D. program, and currently teaches in Aish Dos and Mercaz Teacher Training Programs.

He is the author of twenty personal growth and parenting books and cassette programs, and writes a popular weekly column for Torah Umesorah published in the *Yated Ne'eman*. His most recent books are *Vitamins for the Spirit* and *Speak Up*.

Mr. Shulman is a nationally acclaimed speaker and teacher.

INTRODUCTION

Thoughts are where it is at.

Why?

Because our thoughts determine what we think of ourselves, how we perceive our abilities, how we react to what happens to us, and where we would like to go in life.

To a thinking person ...

... speech begins with thoughts.

... action begins with thoughts.

... religious adherence depends on thoughts.

... change is prefaced by thoughts.

... mistakes are learned by thoughts.

... relationships with others depend on thoughts.

... our happiness depends on thoughts.

Thoughts are the building blocks of our lives because what we do outwardly is but the expression of our inner thoughts.

There is no profound or deep philosophy in this book, rather, easy to understand thoughts that all enjoy — the common denominator being *Thoughts to Build On*.

Each brief chapter can be read in just a few minutes and hopes to give you a different, stimulating thought to mull over in your mind and discuss with your family. To enhance your enjoyment this book, I suggest you use it as a conversation starter with your family. Open to almost any chapter and ask, "What would *you* say about this topic?" or "How would *you* solve this problem?" This should lead to an exciting discussion. You may agree or disagree with a specific approach or suggestion; that's really not important. What is important is that you do independent thinking on the subject at hand and discuss it.

We have chosen three general topics for this book: Parenting, Teaching, and Personal Growth.

Parenting, for many, especially those with large families, is a subject that occupies a disproportionate amount of time, energy, and worry. Parenting skills, until most recently, were thought to come automatically with the firstborn's first cry. We were supposed to do "what came naturally," which probably meant we were to do what our parents did; and if we had a problem on occasion, a quick question to grandmother would provide all the direction needed.

In the last few decades we have been coming to grips with the reality that although our own parenting instincts are adequate most of the time, there are enough times when we need guidance from others. Whether it is because of changing times, family size, working mothers, the influence of the media, or any or all of the above, the bottom line is that parenting has become a subject to which all of us should pay our full attention. I hope that I presented some positive and useful ideas — mostly borrowed — for your consideration.

Teaching is not limited to the *rebbe*, *morah*, or teacher standing at the front of the classroom; rather I have included ideas and suggestions for all of us. In truth, all of us in one way or another are teachers. The *rebbe* teaches formally in the classroom, the rabbi teaches in his sermons and in adult classes, and the parent teaches in casual discussion … but we all teach. So the ideas and suggestions offered here will hopefully be of interest to everyone.

Personal growth is a catchall phrase that is meant to include almost anything that will make us better, that will stimulate growth, that will bring us closer to reaching our many objectives.

In our Yeshiva days we would hear the phrase "*shtigen in lernin*" or "*shtigen in middos*" which, loosely translated, means "to grow, to improve in learning or behavior." We can recall our *rosh yeshiva*, *rebbe*, or *mashgiach* imploring, urging, or challenging — and on occasion demanding of us — to improve! Their message was: "Strive to make this week more productive than last week; strive to make your ethical behavior more refined than last month; strive to make your *davening* this quarter more meaningful than last quarter."

Those of us who leave the walls of the yeshiva can wait in vain for years for someone to challenge us to "*shteig.*" The sad truth is that most of us have to challenge ourselves if we want to achieve.

Just as the entry-level office worker is at first accountable to a boss, and as he goes up the corporate ladder, increasingly accountable to himself, so each of us should become more self-accountable as we mature.

These articles are the result of prodding by Rabbi Joshua Fishman, Executive Vice President of Torah Umesorah. He recognized the need for parents and teachers to discuss relevant topics, and over the years that I was a Torah Umesorah staff member he continually urged me to write.

Rabbi Yaakov Rajchenbach, in his first year as president of Torah Umesorah, suggested that these articles be published in a weekly column in the *Yated Ne'eman*.

I am grateful to Rabbi Fishman, Rabbi Rajchenbach, and Rabbi Pinchos Lipshutz, publisher of *Yated Ne'eman,* for their encouragement and support.

I would like to thank Rabbi and Rebbitzen Yisroel Flam, and my wife Erica, for their help.

Thank you ...

First, I wish to express profound gratitude to Hashem for having given me so much ... life, health, talents, opportunities, a very special family, friends, and community. I am especially blessed to have always been associated with *rosh yeshivas, rabbonim, bnei Torah* and Torah personalities.

My father's *zt"l yiras Shamayim*, integrity, and dedication to Torah is a constant inspiration to me. No doubt, the benevolence Hashems gifts to me is a "*zchus avos*."

I want to express appreciation to the very special people who over the last years have embraced me with concern, support, and true friendship. Each in their own way, in the right time, has helped and inspired me. In many ways, my venture into lecturing and writing was the result of the confidence they had in me.

My family: my wife Erica, our children, and their extended families.

A group of friends who over the years have inspired me: Rabbi Eliezer Goldfischer, Rabbi Moshe Mendel Glustein, Mr. Naftoli Hirsch, Mr. Dovid Singer, Rabbi Hertzel Schechter, and Rabbi Velvel Rosen; and to those good friends who were nifter: Rabbi Moshe Ahron Baumrind, Rabbi Asher Tesser, and Rabbi Hershel Goldwurm, *zt"l*.

My Torah Umesorah family, with special appreciation to Rabbi Joshua Fishman.

My S.E.E.D. family, with special appreciation to Rabbi Joseph Grunfeld of London.

My Mercaz family, with special appreciation to Rabbis Berel and Chaim Wein, and Rabbi Joel Kramer.

My Aish Dos family, with special appreciation to Rabbi Dovid Bernstein.

My Daf Yomi family; my ArtScroll family; my Mesivta Bais Shraga family, with special appreciation to Rabbi Avrohom Greenfeld and Rabbi Moshe Weinberger.

My Yeshiva of Spring Valley family, with special appreciation to Mr. Joseph Kazarnovsky.

My *rebbes* and *chavrusos*, with special appreciation to Rabbi Chaim Rosenberg and Rabbi Shmuel Klein, my "boys club," a tremendous thank you.

It has been my special privilege to have Rabbi and Rebbitzen Yisroel Flam as my dear friends for the past forty years.

A special appreciation to Rabbi J. Fishman, Rabbi Jack Rajchenbach and Rabbi Pinchos Lipshutz for encouraging and sponsoring the Torah Umesorah articles in the *Yated Ne'eman*.

1.

MORAL COMPASS

*R*ecently the term moral compass has become popular. You may find it interesting to discuss this concept with your children.

Do you know what a compass is? Are you able to describe it? It is a device that tells direction by its small metal strip, a needle that always points north. When Hashem created the earth, He placed a magnetic field — like a gigantic magnet — near the North Pole. The pull of this magnetic field is so strong that if you have a small piece of magnetized metal that can spin easily, it will always point toward the north! It makes no difference where you hold this needle — in New York, Chicago, St. Louis, Los Angeles, Miami, Brazil, Europe, or Eretz Yisrael — if the metal is magnetized and can spin freely, it will always point north.

The compass has been the true friend of everyone who has traveled across water, in a forest, in a desert — anywhere that had no marked road or highways. The compass always works: It is unaffected by where it is or who is holding it. You can just imagine how many people found their way out of life-threatening situations because of this small *chesed* — this miraculous creation of Hashem.

Since the compass works on the principle of magnetism, the one thing that disables the compass is a distracting magnetic field. For example, if a compass is near a telephone, or an electric motor, the magnetic fields created by these items will throw the compass off. Instead of pointing north, it may point to the west or east. Sometimes, if the competing magnetic field is strong, it will make the compass needle just spin around aimlessly. The compass becomes useless: it can't give us any true direction, and even worse, it may mislead us.

In a special way which we cannot easily understand, the *neshamah* of a Jew, the Torah, and Hashem are one. They all have something in common.

Using the example of a compass, it might very well be that the pure *neshamah*, because it is part of *Hakadosh Boruch Hu*, always points to the *Toras Emes*, which is also part of *Hakadosh Boruch Hu*. Just as the magnetized needle always points to the north because of the magnetic attraction, so too the pure *neshamah* is attracted to the Torah.

We can take this thought one step further. Just as the needle has to be magnetized to respond to the magnetic pull of the North Pole, so too the *neshamah* has to be embraced by Torah and mitzvos until it will automatically always point to the truth — the Torah.

When this is so, the person himself will become a moral compass! He will not be affected by where he is, with whom he is, or how big the temptation is. If he has absorbed the Torah's commandment, "Do not steal," it will make no difference if the opportunity is to steal $100, $1,000, a million dollars, or even a single penny. His moral compass always points to the Torah, which states what is right and what is wrong.

Just as a magnetic compass can be "thrown off" and point us in wrong directions, so too a person's moral compass can be "thrown off." If he develops inappropriate friendships with people who do things that are wrong, or if he reads, watches, or listens to inappropriate things, his moral compass will experience interference. Just as magnetic interference makes the compass needle point to a direction which is not north, in the same way bad influences will deflect a person's moral compass away from the Torah's truths.

2.
BILL GATES

ou're in the house of a successful contractor in a Midwestern community. He is an Orthodox Jew who over the past ten years has been minimally supportive of the local *kollel*.

The head of the *kollel*, a respected *talmid chacham*, and its lay leader president, a prominent businessman, are in desperate need of several thousand dollars to make this month's payroll. The two men decided to visit the contractor to try to persuade him to make a major donation.

After some small talk, the conversation focuses on the *kollel*. The president points out that since the *kollel* came to this community, more than thirty men have enrolled in a serious learning program and a number of children are coming to learn on Sundays as well as on several evenings. He goes on to proudly point out additional memorable accomplishments. He also lists several programs and projects that *kollel* members have initiated for the men, women, and children of the community.

The contractor hardly speaks but his body language says he is uncomfortable and possibly annoyed by the reciting of the long list of accomplishments. Finally, with a glint in his eye and a hint of a smile on his lips, he says, "Your eleven men have been learning for years … have you produced one Rogatchover (an exceptionoal genius who lived in the 1800's) … or have one of your *kollel* men written a *sefer* like Reb Moshe Feinstein *zt"l*? Your *kollel* men are just average *talmidei chachamim* … why should I support them?"

The *rosh kollel* is taken aback by the brazenness of the questions, and to give himself some time to think of a proper response, he decides to engage the gentleman in conversation on a different track. "We'll get to your question in a few minutes," he said, "but in the meantime may I ask you some questions about how you got into your present line of work?"

This one question opens a whole flood of memories and stories about how after he graduated college he took an office job, but also started to do small home repair in his spare time. Slowly, he gained more experience in the construction industry and after struggling for a few years went full time into building homes. He now builds between ten and twenty houses a year.

The *rosh kollel* had an interesting thought. He gently asked if he could be so bold as to assume that building and selling ten to twenty homes a year produced an income in very general terms of between $500,000 and a million dollars. The contractor agreed to these figures. Then the *talmid chacham* asked the contractor if he had any idea of how much money Bill Gates earns in a year? They reasoned on an approximate income of several hundred million dollars. Then the *rosh kollel* asked the following question: How can you justify going to work to earn a few hundred thousand dollars, when in the same period of time Mr. Gates earns several hundreds of millions?

There was a long pause, then the *rosh kollel* softly said, "When it comes to earning a living, we each have to do that which we can do. We have to feed and provide for our families. We each do our best. It would be foolhardy not to work and go hungry just because we can earn only thousands and can't earn millions like someone else!"

After a long thoughtful silence the contractor wrote a check for the month's payroll.

3.

THE SON I NEVER HAD

A true story: A friend of mine who spent thirty years building a prestigious Yeshiva Day School told me that one afternoon he went to visit a neighbor who was quite ill. This wealthy man had lived in the same area as my friend for years, and they had a cordial relationship.

This is the story he told me: The sick man was in the advanced stage of a fatal disease, but was fully coherent and wanted to talk. During the conversation, my friend casually mentioned something about the school he headed, to which the sick man responded, "I want you to know that I have watched you over the last few decades, and your accomplishments have really inspired me! You know that

I never had a son, but had I had a son, I would have wanted him to do exactly what you have done. In fact," he continued, "in many ways you're the son I never had."

He went on to explain that although he was a very successful businessman, his heart and soul were always in *chinuch*. Teaching children Torah was his first love. He had watched the way my friend struggled to build a small Torah school, slowly gaining acceptance in the community. This school had tens of graduates in prestigious positions in cities around the world.

They spoke for another few minutes. My friend bid him well, and went home. A few weeks later the wealthy man died.

The statement, "You were the son I never had," rang in my friend's ears for weeks. The man who said this was an honest man not given to excessive exaggeration, and my friend believed him and understood what he was trying to convey.

What my friend could not understand was where this wealthy man was all those years. There were times when a word of praise would have meant so much! While he had always sent in a yearly donation to the school, he had never expressed a word of encouragement, never sent a note of support!

To hear, "You're the son I never had," from the lips of a dying man is a powerful experience, and a tremendous ego trip, but he would gladly have traded it for a few words of praise during those struggling years.

One of the cardinal rules of life is that, for the most part, we cannot read other people's minds. We can only judge them by their words and actions. Even if we could read their thoughts, if their actions contradict their thoughts, we would not believe them.

If a neighbor never invited me to his home in three years, didn't respond to my invitations or *mishloach manos,* did not visit me when I was sick, and did not express any other sign of friendship, how meaningful would it be to hear him tell me "in his *heart"* I was really his good friend!

In all relationships between husbands and wives, parents and children, teachers and students, neighbors and friends, we need to say it, express it, and do it. Just thinking it does not convey our feelings.

We can go one step further. When a non-Orthodox Jew says, "I'm a good Jew at heart," we automatically think, "When the Almighty says, 'Loving Me is expressed by doing mitzvos,' your good intentions and good heart are not enough."

In the same way, our good feeling toward someone needs to be expressed to be meaningful. Don't waste decades withholding your good feelings toward someone; rather, put them into words and actions.

4.
THE BIG QUESTION

he phone rings at 9 o'clock to confirm the 9:30 appointment. Promptly at 9:30 they knock on the door.

You have known them casually over the years. He is close to forty, a nice *frum* man. He had gone to *yeshiva* and learned for two years in *kollel,* then became a computer analyst. He *davens* at a small *minyan* and is one of the original members of the *Daf Yomi shiur* there.

The wife is a graduate of Bais Yaakov who spent a year in seminary, taught for two years, got married, and continued teaching for the next three years. Since then she has become a full-time mother and homemaker, volunteering some of her time to local *tzedakos.*

Their six children, ages three to sixteen, are in various yeshivos and Bais Yaakovs, all average to above-average students. If you had to categorize this family, you would say that they are really nice people who enjoy a good marriage, have a wonderful family, are *bnei Torah,* and are community-minded.

Three weeks ago they received a letter informing them that they had won a tremendous amount of money in an international lottery. They had bought the ticket six months ago to satisfy the request of a neighbor's child. At first they thought it was a hoax; but after confirming it with their lawyer, district attorney, and bank president, they were assured that it was legitimate. They have been guaranteed that in three months the full amount of $49,990,597 (that reads 49 million-plus dollars), tax free, will be deposited into their account.

This couple knows that the history of most people who suddenly and unexpectedly received large amounts of money is sad. Individuals or families who won or inherited big money, especially if they had no experience in handling such sums, found for the most part that the money ruined their health, marriages, friendships, and careers, and in just a few years the money was lost. A considerable number of these people became addicted to alcohol or other drugs. Their lives became void of any meaning. Many of these people later viewed their "big win" as a curse. In looking back, many of the winners honestly said they wished it had never happened.

Having said that, the couple's question to you is, "What do we do?" They greatly appreciate their present lifestyle, values, and spiritual achievement. They live modestly, struggle with the usual problems, but could easily use a larger home, a new car, a family trip to Eretz Yisrael. Looking down the road a few years, they can see supporting some of their children in *kollel*, an apartment in Yerushalayim, and so on. After all, they were given the money as a gift to use, weren't they?

On the other hand, they truly don't want to become indulged, pampered, or coddled people. They have worked hard to attain the special qualities of their family, and don't want to trade these in for wealth. They don't want to place themselves or their children "at risk." How can they accept the money and not change?

They have come to you as a trusted, respected advisor. To date, no one (except the few professionals who are sworn to secrecy) knows of the win. They have all their options open, and they are anxious to be advised. Any suggestions?

～⁂～

Addendum to "The Big Question:"

The most frequent answers have been:

1. I only wish that I had the problem.
2. They have to come for weekly consultations at $50,000 per session … for twenty sessions.
3. To really understand the problem, I need to personally experience it. Please direct-deposit $5 million in my account.

～⁂～

Seriously, what do we tell them?

5.

GRIST FOR THE MILL

id you ever hear the expression "grist for the mill"? Many people who have heard it and occasionally use it don't know its origin. Once upon a time, after wheat was gathered and dried, it had to be ground into flour. The most effective way to grind wheat prior to the mechanical age was to grind it between two heavy millstones.

When the wheat kernels were placed on the bottom millstone and another heavy millstone was placed on top, the kernels would be crushed instead of ground. The action of the two stones would be smooth. Friction and abrasion were needed to do the job. To enable the millstones to grind instead of crush, it was necessary to add gravel to the kernels. The gravel — known as grist — rubbed against the grain as the mill wheel passed over them, and ground the kernels into flour. The flour was then sifted, and all the gravel was removed. The end product was perfectly smooth, ground flour.

A farmer who brought his wheat to be ground for the first time and had never seen the process could indignantly protest, "Why are you throwing gravel into my wheat? I do not want any gravel in my flour!" If the miller accommodated his request and used no grist, the farmer would get crushed grain, and then complain, "I wanted ground flour, not crushed flour!"

The principle was relatively simple. If you wanted high-quality flour, you had to add grist to the mill.

This idea opens the opportunity to explain a concept in *hashkafah* — Torah viewpoint — in an interesting way that can easily be understood.

You may have heard someone say, "Just as everything was going along so smoothly ... this had to happen!" A person may have worked hard to open a new business, and just as the business begins to prosper, he falls and breaks a leg. He is put out for three weeks, and then can only function in a limited way for the next two months. Or a person who is slowly recovering from some personal trauma is suddenly faced with another crisis. You can almost hear these people say, "Just as things were going so smoothly ... this had to happen!"

We believe that Hashem has a specific role, purpose, and design for each and every person. Whatever the reasons are, Hashem wants each of us to reach a certain position in our service to Him, and to achieve this Hashem gives us life, health, and all our needs. When life goes along smoothly, when everything fits into place, when there is little resistance in any area of our lives, we, like the wheat kernels, may not produce the results that Hashem wants from us, and for us.

Challenges, problems, trials and tribulations are the "grist" of life, intended to make us better people, to make our neshamos more sensitive, more pure. Every *nisayon,* or challenge, can be viewed as a terrible, unnecessary piece of "gravel" in our wheat kernels or grist to make our *neshamos* pure, and desirable.

It is Hashem's province to decide when, how, and to whom to give a *nisayon*; it our choice how to see it.

It has been wisely said, "Comfort zones are most often expanded by discomfort."

6.

"HARK!"

I will allow the reader to make his own observation on the following letter.

Dear Mr. Shulman:

I had read an article that you wrote about driving a car as a way to make a kiddush Hashem. It was especially meaningful, and we spent an hour discussing ways to do this and to avoid driving in a way that causes discomfort and chillul Hashem.

Several weeks later, my wife and I went out of our way to visit some old friends, but each time they weren't home. Last Friday I drove into the center of town, and as I was turning into a side street

I saw my old friend walking. I left the car almost blocking the street, ran out of the car to greet my friend, and got into a conversation. Traffic was going around my car, and occasionally I got a dirty look for blocking the street, but both of us were into a deep conversation and neither of us saw or heard the commotion. It was only when a lady took the time to stop, lower her window, and tell me in no uncertain terms what she thought of me that I realized the chillul Hashem I was creating. I got into the car and tried to find a place to park. To add insult to injury, the cassette I was listening to at that moment was Rabbi Salomon, the Lakewood Mashgiach, explaining that chillul Hashem occurs when someone who is even perceived *as a ben Torah does something improper.*

So here I was. I had read the article, I had discussed the article, I was listening to the cassette ... and none of these had any bearing on what I was doing! My only consolation was, "Hark, I hear the cannon roar!" [Rabbi Frand, in his Chofetz Chaim Heritage Foundation Video Tisha B'av message, told the story of an actor who had just one simple line to say on stage. After two weeks of rehearsals, when the moment came and the actors were finally on stage in front of an audience, he flubbed his line. Instead of saying, "Hark, I hear the cannon roar," he was so flustered at hearing the noise of the cannon that he blurted out, "What in the world was that?"]

I told my children the story, and we all had a great laugh. I then told them that sometimes it is hard for a person to internalize a concept and translate it into action. I hope they get the message.

I thought you might enjoy the story.

Sincerely,
Chaim K.

Thank you, Reb Chaim, for your interesting letter. My only comment is to commend you for discussing it with your children.

It is important that children realize that adults, even parents, struggle with personal growth. Children often mistakenly think that their parents have always been good, kind, and *frum*. They don't realize that the level of achievement that their parents enjoy today is a result of growth, struggle, failure, and further growth.

"Share this lesson as a powerful lesson and example for children."

7.

ICE CREAM

he Mt. Ivy cottages represent the best one could want in spiritual and physical pleasures. There are forty-five summer cottages situated on this magnificent one-hundred acre property, which once was the summer home of a tycoon. When he died, his estate sold the property to a group of Orthodox Jews. With a few thousand dollars, the centrally located playhouse became a *shul*, a fence was erected around the pool, and a small dock was built for the lake.

The group who bought the land understood that, although they were all on the same economic and social level, in the next decade or two the status of the residents would likely change. To insure that the quality of spiritual life in the colony would remain the same, they developed rules regarding the *shul,* the size of new cottages that could be built, *tzenius,* television, and the like.

For years these people have lived harmoniously, despite their varied backgrounds. That is, until the coming of the ice cream man. Now, for the first time that anyone can remember, there are two opposing factions, and they can't come to any resolution. They don't want to vote on it because they know a vote is devisive. They prefer to work it out.

Because they are good people who have been friends for years and who value their friendship highly, they have decided to ask a smart person what to do. They have decided to seek advice from … you!

Here are all the viewpoints in this situation:

a) Joe Silverspoon is a very nice young man of nineteen. Joe is a friendly, outgoing person who has an entrepreneurial drive. He rents an ice cream van and sells *cholov Yisrael* ice cream to children in the various cottages.

Mt. Ivy cottages are on private property, so Joe has asked permission to come at 4 o'clock every afternoon. He has been doing this for two weeks and has quite a following, with nearly all the children buying ice cream every day. Four o'clock has become ice cream time!

b) Mr. Phil Goldstein represents a group of cottage owners who have no reason to stop Joe from coming in. In fact, it saves many of them a trip into town, a convenience they appreciate.

c) Mrs. Gray represents a group of cottage owners who feel that Joe's presence is creating a new problem in their midst. Some families can't afford ice cream every afternoon. In addition, even for those who can afford it, she feels that parents should not have to deal with the constant pressure of having to say "no" to their children. Her point is that all the children did very well without the daily ice cream. Why teach them a new *ta'avah*, a new desire?

So here, in short, you have the three positions.

Mr. Goldstein says that a responsible parent should teach his child how to control his desires. The whole group shouldn't have to suffer because of these children. Mrs. Gray says that we don't need to create new desires. Not all the parents know how to control their children's desires, nor do these parents want to be turned into the "bad guys." Joe only wants to earn a few dollars.

Judges, what do you say?

❧

As a postscript: Mike Bronn called. He sells cookies, and wants permission to come every morning at 11. What are you going to tell him?

8.
CARPOOLING FOR SCHOOL
Part One

"Carpooling" is one of those trigger words that, depending on where you live, can send shock waves through parents of schoolchildren. It conjures up images of frustration, complex logistical arrangements, and weariness.

In the morning some children are slow to wake up and get ready. We may start a few minutes late, but we still have to pick up all the other children and be in school on time. When children come out of school some are in a daze and function like zombies, while others are like a released spring, full of energy and fury.

In addition, packing children of different ages, temperaments, and personalities, along with their bulging briefcases, into a cramped space is a significant ordeal. Add rain, dusk, or darkness, and you have all the ingredients of a major Excedrin headache.

Let us discuss carpooling in the most rational way possible, and try to find some ways to make it safer, easier, more comfortable, and less frustrating.

The History of Carpooling
(or How Did We Ever Get Ourselves Into This Mess?)

There are three types of school transportation communities:

1. Large cities where, for the most part, children walk to school, though parents carpool on occasion.

2. Communities whose schools do provide transportation, but who rely on carpooling on Sundays, legal holidays, for *mishmor*, and extracurricular activities.

3. Communities where no public transportation is provided and children have to be driven to schools at all times. Chicago, Baltimore, and Southfield are examples of such communities.

In a country that provides free education and free bus transportation, we have chosen to send our sons and daughters to yeshiva day schools. Each of us feels to the core of his being that the prime obligation and privilege of a Jewish parent is to teach his children Torah and a Torah value system. We make enormous financial sacrifices to do this, with some families paying tens of thousands of dollars in tuition each year, comprising 20 percent (and more) of their total income! More than anything else, we want our children to remain loyal to our heritage and become true *bnei* and *bnos Yisrael*.

Fifty years ago when someone bought a home, he chose one within a few blocks of the school which his children would attend, so that they could walk.

Over the years, as Orthodox families moved to the newer sections of the city and to the suburbs, new schools had to be built. Because of economics and zoning considerations, the residential areas and the schools were often far from each other. Moreover, for safety reasons, walking to school was not always a desirable option. Thus, a new phenomenon occurred — driving children to school. As a matter of convenience and economy, the idea of carpooling as way of life eventually developed.

What may start out as a pleasant ride to school with one's own children becomes for many a pressured, tension-filled burden. Carpooling can become the pivot around which the whole day revolves. ("I can't go on Monday or Tuesday morning or Thursday afternoon — I carpool!") It can also become a wedge that divides neighbors and friends ("Rivka joined Chana's carpool!") and may even develop into a status symbol ("Finally, we made it into 'The Carpool!' ").

The Talmud tells us that learning Gemara merits a unique reward which is unobtainable in any other way.

Notwithstanding the many mitzvos a person has done, this one merit is accessed only by the physical toil of learning, the "give and take" of Gemara. The Talmud then asks, "If so, how do women, who do not learn Gemara, merit this reward?" And it answers, "By taking their children to and from yeshiva, and by enabling their husbands to go to yeshiva, and [patiently] waiting for them."

Perhaps we should step back for a moment to realize that when a father or a mother drive children to learn Torah (read "carpool"), they are not just in the "transportation" business, but rather are physically participating in a mitzvah so closely identified with the actual learning of Gemara that the Talmud assigns them the very same special reward! Perhaps the reason carpooling is so difficult and frustrating, is because it is so great a mitzvah! I don't mean to imply that this perspective will cause all the frustrations to magically disappear ... but it can raise in our own eyes the mitzvah-value of this task and allow us to view it as a worthwhile achievement.

9.
CARPOOLING FOR SCHOOL
Part Two

In the early years of Bais Medrosh Elyon in Monsey, the yeshiva needed a cook. Rabbi Mendlowitz *zt"l* hired a couple who had miraculously survived the war and had come to New York penniless and heartbroken. Although Reb Leib Apfeldorfer had been an extremely wealthy man in Czechoslovakia, his desperate need to earn a living led him to become a cook in the yeshiva. Over several decades, he and his wife became beloved role models to all the *bochurim*. In fact, Rabbi Nosson Scherman, who was a student in the yeshiva at that time, wrote an article in Olomeinu, Torah Umesorah's children's magazine, about the

Apfeldorfers, in which he mentioned a rosh yeshiva telling a student, "Reb Leib is a living *Shulchan Arach*; there is so much to learn from him."

That article came to mind when I started thinking about carpooling, because it is an excellent example of the notion that we teach when we least think we are teaching. I know that the last thing a carpooling father or mother needs is the knowledge that they are also "teaching" during their driving, but the fact of the matter is that their small charges are absorbing everything that is happening during the car ride, just as the yeshiva students unconsciously absorbed values from the cook and his wife.

Here are some practical considerations to make carpooling easier, smoother, and less of a hassle:

1. Allow enough time at home to start carpool on time. The problem begins when you leave the house in the morning just a few minutes late, or don't allow enough time in the afternoon to get to school at dismissal. The single factor contributing most to the pressure of carpooling is being rushed. People who schedule their day so tightly that they have just 30 minutes to go from downtown to the school invariably find that traffic or weather turns the 30-minute trip into a 40-minute trip.

2. Allow for more time on the pickup route. If you need 21 minutes under ideal conditions to pick up children from four houses and get to school, allow 25 to 30 minutes,

because rarely, if ever, are conditions ideal! If your pickup schedule is so tight that a child who walks s-l-o-w-l-y from his house to the car sends you into a frenzy ... your schedule is just too tight.

3. Insist on safety procedures. We have to develop a mindset that, regardless how rushed or how late we are, we can never compromise on safety. Measures include seat belts, the maximum number of children we will transport, and a safe driving speed, etc.

4. Assign seats. The last thing you need at pickup time is a car full of feuding children. Who sits next to the window is traditionally the spark that ignites a good fight. Even if you have to reassign seats every month, it may help.

5. Develop rules that everyone agrees upon. Have a clear understanding of what children need to do in order to be "ready," such as having their coats on, their briefcases ready, and their lunches and snacks packed. Perhaps even write a checklist for them. Likewise, when school is over, specify where and when the children should meet you.

6. Project a pleasant, happy disposition. Even if you are in a rush, take a moment to change your disposition from hurried and harrassed to smiling and pleasant. Show children that you can be pleasant even when you're under pressure.

7. Create a nice atmosphere. You might consider playing a calming cassette or an interesting story cassette. You may want to provide an occasional surprise, such as a snack.

8. Don't lose yourself. If you vent your (justified) anger on the "stupid" person who blocked all the cars, can you expect a child to act differently? The few minutes you patiently wait and the courtesy you afford another driver are a worthwhile lesson.

Years from now your children may not remember what they learned in school on one particuclar day, but they may well remember the parent who carpooled and was able to smile and project joy in spite of all the problems.

10.
MY RABBI

The group of Yeshiva boys had been on a Torah Umesorah S.E.E.D. program for the last number of weeks. They had taught adults and children, learned by themselves, and thoroughly enjoyed the opportunity to get to know a new community. The ten boys and the two couples were all from the New York area, and for most it was their first time in a picturesque New England town.

Now they were about to go home. The community had planned a farewell banquet at which the host — the principal of the local Yeshiva, and a good friend of mine — as well as two S.E.E.D. students, spoke.

After all the official speeches, the S.E.E.D. boys made a presentation to the principal in appreciation for his hosting the program and for making the group comfortable. As a token of their appreciation, the boys presented him with an Israeli olive-wood wall display which had a clock, several biblically inspired designs, and an empty picture frame.

The principal graciously accepted the gift, and a few days later hung it in the school office. In the picture frame he placed a beautiful color picture of his *rebbe* and mentor, Rav Pam, smiling broadly.

Several weeks later a parent of a student came into the office to discuss a problem regarding his child. The father noticed the wooden display and asked the principal about it. The principal told him about the boys and the presentation at the farewell dinner. When questioned about Rav Pam's picture, the rabbi explained that Rav Pam was his *rebbe* and that he often sought his counsel in halachic and other issues. The rabbi felt that it was important for everyone to have a *rebbe* who is a counselor and guide; the longer one is away from the yeshiva, the more important a *rebbe* is, because as time goes on, we lose the idealism and inspiration of the yeshiva days.

The principal then asked the parent, "Whose picture would you put into the frame?"

The father stared at the frame for what seemed like a long time, and then in all seriousness said, "I would put a mirror into the frame."

When you hear a story like this you don't know if you should laugh or cry.

Even as we grow older, we will still find it important and necessary to ask questions and seek advice from those who were our *rebbeim* in our youth, or from an older *rebbe* or rabbi. However, as the older generation slowly fades away and we age, we find ourselves facing people who are our peers, or perhaps even younger than we are. Asking them for advice is very difficult.

Consider the problem of a person who moves from his old neighborhood to the suburbs, and suddenly finds the Rabbi of his new synagogue to be a *yungerman* twenty years his junior. There is suddenly a great temptation not to have any *sh'ailos* and not to ask for any advice from this young rabbi, and instead to look to the mirror for help. Yet the instructions of the Mishnah are clear.

The new young rabbi may not have the decades of experience or the depth of learning of your former rav, yet the Mishnah teaches, "Make a *rebbe* for yourself." Because, among other reasons, he does have an objectivity that you can't have, and as a rav he is blessed with special Providential assistance to answer questions correctly, it important to ask him.

The instruction of the Mishnah, "Make a *rebbe* for yourself," doesn't have an age limit. It does not say, "Youngsters should have a *rebbe*." Rather, it is meant for all of us, at all times, and all places.

The real danger of not having a rav is that instead, you'll look for advice in a mirror.

II.

INFORMATION OVERLOAD

good teacher spends as much time planning what not to teach as he does planning what to teach!

It's interesting to note how people receive information. Tell a person one or two pieces of information and perhaps he will understand and remember it. Tell him the same information and add another ten points, and you can be certain that you have considerably reduced his ability to remember any part of it! The reason is simple: information overload.

The word "overload" brings to mind an electrical outlet into which appliances are plugged. A toaster, heater, lamp, microwave, and radio are all plugged into the same outlet. You turn on the toaster, then the heater, and then the lamp. So far so good; they all work. Now you turn on the microwave and the fuse blows ... and there is no electricity for any of the appliances! When you overload a circuit, you cause a fuse to blow, and all current stops.

"Information overload" happens often when I ask a question of a person who is really knowledgeable. Instead of getting just a simple answer, one that I can understand and digest, the person floods me with a torrent of facts, figures, rules, and exceptions ... making sure that even the simple facts become eclipsed.

The Gemara expresses this idea beautifully when it says, "More than the calf wants to suck its mother's milk, the cow wants to give the calf milk." *Rebbes, morahs,* and teachers who are truly knowledgeable tend to want to share the knowledge with their students more than the students want to learn it.

A book designer has many ways to slow down the delivery of information to the reader. He may choose a larger typeface and shorter lines with much white space around the type so that the reader has to grapple with less information on each page. He can divide the material into chapters so it will be easier to digest. Ultimately, the overriding control of the flow of ideas is in the hands of the reader, who can choose at any time to stop reading. He can put it down for few minutes to rethink an idea, or to review the last few pages.

All of these methods of controlling the rate of information delivery are unavailable to the teacher, the lecturer, or the parent. If we pile it on too high, or too fast, we may lose our effectiveness. We have to be careful that in our desire to teach, we don't overload the students' circuits. All of us, teachers and parents alike, have to spoonfeed information in small bites until the child is ready for more.

The child or adult who is being flooded with information may not have the opportunity to say, "Stop! It's enough," although their body language may say it. But when you overload their circuits you risk having them not absorb anything. More is not always better.

12.
TEACHING OPPORTUNITIES

*I*n the previous chapter we discussed "information overload," which happens when we are given too much information all at once.

One of the areas where I have witnessed information overload is in the field of finances. If I ask a knowledgeable person a simple question about finances, an avalanche of facts, charts, figures, and words which I don't understand immediately falls on me. In just a few minutes, I'm sorry I asked.

All of this crossed my mind when I nonchalantly asked a young *choson* where he intended to invest his *chasunah* money. He gave me a wide-eyed look, as if to say, "Invest? I haven't any idea, other than to keep our money in our checking account." He asked me to teach him a little about it. In a moment of weakness (he happens to be the son of a lifelong friend, and they are a charming young couple) I agreed. The conditions were that both husband and wife come, take notes, and pass a written test at the end of the hour (just kidding about the test!).

Since I am far from being knowledgeable in the investment field, I decided to ask some people who are, but I promised myself to use my teaching expertise to explain this material in an easy-to-understand way.

Why do I tell you this in a column dedicated to teaching and parenting? Because I find most parents really want to teach their children the basics of investing, but for some reason don't. Perhaps many parents don't know how to break down such a complex subject into easy-to-understand, bite-size pieces of information.

I must tell you that after speaking to a number of experts, I still find the subject intimidating. Nevertheless, I have given considerable thought about how to simplify investing, and I offer it here because of its *chesed* value. Why *chesed*, you may ask? The answer is that if you can teach a person how to invest a relatively small amount of money in a relatively safe way, he may have money to dignify his later years, and that is a great *chesed*.

Before I move on to the nuts and bolts of our subject, I would like to preface it with some general comments.

The Teaching Opportunity

When I was a first-grade *rebbe*, I once visited a friend whose son, now a "big third-grader," had been in my class. When I walked in, I saw my former student lying on the floor glued to the latest issue of Olomeinu, Torah Umesorah's popular children's magazine. I remember how difficult a student this boy had been and I asked the father if he had improved. The father told me that the boy still resists learning in class but, surprisingly, loves to read stories. "Somehow," the father went on to explain, "a story which is not presented in a formal setting is easier for him to accept."

There are children who resist accepting *hashkafah*, Torah values, when presented by an official *rebbe* or *morah* yet are ready to "hear" these very same *hashkafos* when presented in a different way. One example would be a camp counselor walking his bunk, who stops to discuss whether a person is allowed to break off a tree branch for no purpose. If the counselor can uses this opportunity to discuss the greatness of Hashem at a totally unexpected time and place, the child's defenses are not up. If the counselor uses this "teaching moment" to its full potential, he can interest even the hard-to-reach child.

Teaching *hashkafos* while discussing investing offers the parent just such a unique "Teaching Opportunity."

I ask that you read the following chapters on "Attitude Toward Money" with this in mind.

13.
ATTITUDE TOWARD MONEY
Part One

In the last chapter I set a challenge for myself and my readers to explain a complex subject such as investing in simple, easy-to-understand segments so that parents can teach these ideas to their children.

I think we should begin by understanding for ourselves the reasons teaching about investing is so important.

In addition to the obvious desire to teach children important life skills, there are three basic *hashkafos* that a parent can teach along with this subject:

a) Whose money is it? The Torah perception is that all the money that comes from the labor, mind, or industry of a person is a gift of the Almighty. It may be the work of the farmer who cultivated and harvested the crop, but who, if not the Almighty, gave the farmer the understanding of how to plant, the energy to do the work, the seed, rich earth, rain, and sunshine to make it grow?

When the *pasuk* says, "The silver and gold is Mine," it is meant in the most literal terms. All wealth in whatever form it is — gold, silver, land, stocks, tenure, or ideas — belongs to the Almighty.

Giving 10 percent of our earnings to *tzedakah* is a mitzvah that has to be taught by parents and practiced. It is a mitzvah that has to overcome the natural tendency of a child (or adult) to say, "I worked for it, I earned it … I want it all." We must teach a child that Jewish thought is just the opposite: All belongs to Hashem, Who has allowed us to be the guardians of the money and to distribute it to the poor, only after which we provide for our own needs.

The most painless way to give *tzedakah* is to place 10 percent of the money in a separate account as soon as it is earned. Then, when a check is written on your "charity account," it isn't your money; rather, it is as if you're the *gabbai* of a *tzedakah* fund. When a treasurer of a charity fund writes a check, it doesn't hurt. It isn't his money, he didn't earn it, he can't spend it … so giving it away is painless.

In practical terms, when a child earns $10 and gives $1 to *tzedakah*, he can spend the remaining money as he pleases, but he should be encouraged not to waste it or spend it on junk. True, it is the child's and he earned it, but it is still the Almighty's and should be spent appropriately. Big words for small children? Perhaps, but we don't have to teach all of it at once. What we are discussing is a goal, an objective, not an immediate short-term lesson.

b) Learning to save one's money demonstrates a person's concern with the future. While it is true that no one can control the future, which is totally in the hands of the Almighty, we are instructed to prepare for it.

When our sages teach us, "He who prepares on Erev Shabbos has what to eat on Shabbos," they are referring to much more than the physical cooking and baking for Shabbos. Our rabbis are also saying that the person who prepares in this world by doing mitzvos will reap the benefits in the future world — the world that is called "total Shabbos." If we stop to think of it, we will realize that so much of our belief system is based on the concept that we do today for tomorrow.

While developing a savings plan to save a few dollars each month is basically a materialistic concept, it gives the parent an opportunity to introduce the young child to the fact that mature people always look ahead. Shlomo HaMelech says, "Go learn from the ant," and the commentaries say this refers to the ants' habit of working during the summer to put away for the winter.

This may be the perfect moment to discuss *bitachon* — trust in Hashem — and the need to provide for one's family. (Among many sources, see Rabbi Moshe Feinstein *zt"l* regarding the purchase of life insurance.)

c) Saving money teaches children the need for self-discipline. All savings and investing is based on the practice of putting away money on a regular basis. If the child is allowed to spend all the money he earns or receives as an allowance or a gift, he is being taught to "live up" to his income instead of "living below" it.

The child, then the young adult, then the adult who has no appreciation for saving — and who has never disciplined himself not to buy whatever he wants, even if he has the money — is headed for disaster.

14.
ATTITUDE TOWARD MONEY
Part Two

*L*ast chapter we began to teach the complicated subject of investing in a simple way, by limiting the amount of information to small "bites."

I am sure that I will be accused of oversimplifying the subject, but we can always fill in more information for the student who is ready for it. I think overloading someone with too much information, with the risk that it may turn him off, is a far greater concern than the problem of too little information. Our intent is not to make the student an expert at this point, but rather to stimulate his desire to learn more.

The first point we made in our discussion of money was the importance of teaching a child the need to save. As the wise saying goes (after setting aside *tzedakah*), pay yourself first.

An interesting observation that a friend made about the giving of *tzedakah* applies equally to savings. The young child has to be taught that he has to give a dime from every dollar, and a dollar from every ten, to *tzedakah*. Life experience shows that the more money a person earns, the harder it is to part with it. To make giving *tzedakah* a habit even when you are earning much money, you have to make it part and parcel of the process now. When you receive or earn money, you immediately and automatically give *tzedakah*.

The same mindset can also be taught regarding savings. Whenever you receive or earn money, after giving *tzedakah*, you save or invest. This "automatic reflex" can become the difference between a lifetime of having or a lifetime of lacking.

When the amount of money we are saving warrants it, we can divide our savings to serve two separate objectives.

The child can open one account to save for some large purchase such as a musical instrument, sports equipment, or trip that involves considerable expense. When the child accrues enough savings to purchase the object, you have taught him an important lesson: You will enjoy the benefits of savings. We don't want him to think that all savings are for some nebulous, unknown future.

The second account which we open for him should be targeted toward that faraway future. This is the opportunity to teach a child that time is the investor's greatest ally.

Now we are ready for the next point: What do we do with our savings?

1. Inflation eats away savings. If a person put $1,000 away in a mattress or safe-deposit box ten years ago, today it has only $600 dollars worth of buying power. Why? Because the bottle of milk that cost $1 ten years ago costs $1.60 today; the apartment that rented for $600 a month ten years ago costs $1,000 a month today.

Since the purpose of money is to buy things, we measure the value of money by how much we can buy with it. So if you put away $1,000 ten years ago when it could have bought you 1,000 bottles of milk, and today it will only buy you 625 bottles, your money has lost value.

The loss of buying power every year is called inflation. Even a small yearly inflation of 3 percent or 4 percent will eat away at any money you save. So you have to find a way to overcome the consuming power of inflation.

A bank will pay you to use your money. If a bank will pay you 3, 4, or 5 percent to use your money for a year, will that help you keep ahead of inflation?

If a bank pays you 3 percent at the end of one year, your $1,000 will be worth $1,030. If a bank pays you 4 percent, you will get $1,040 and at 5 percent you will get $1,050. Will you beat inflation?

The answer depends on how much inflation ate away from your money that year. If inflation was 4 percent and you earned 4 percent, you broke even.

It has been said that inflation is a wonderful way to live in a more expensive neighborhood without moving. It's a great joke but a real problem if we don't provide a plan to deal with it.

15.
ATTITUDE TOWARD MONEY
Part Three

This is a continuation of the last chapter, trying to teach the complicated subject of investing in a simple way, by limiting the amount of information to bite-size "doses."

The first point we made was that inflation eats away at savings. So if you put away $1,000, in a year it's worth only $970, and in ten years it is worth only $600.

We then discussed the bank that paid 3 percent interest a year, giving us at the end of the year $1,030. This brings us to the second concept.

2. Taxes take away about one-third of all earnings. The government takes about one out of every three dollars that your money earns that year.

We gave a simple example of $1,000 put into a savings account in a bank, which earns $30 in interest. The government takes away $10 of that interest. So between inflation that could eat away 3 percent, 4 percent, 5 percent, or more a year, and taxes that take away one-third of all earnings each year, we won't be doing so well with our $30.

These are two negative factors that reduce the earnings of our $1,000. Now let's focus on some concepts that will increase the earning power.

3. The magic of compound interest helps. One of the most exciting insights in understanding investing is the fact that the interest of money is compounded. That simply means every year, interest earns interest.

You invest $1,000 at 5 percent. At the end of one year it is worth $1,050. But at the end of two years it is worth $1,102.50; (The first year's interest is $50. The second year's interest is another $50. And in addition, the second year you earned $2.50 (5 percent) on the first year's interest! Interest on interest.) at the end of three years it is worth $1,157; and at the end of five years $1,283.

That may not seem like a lot of money, but if we let the same $1,000 stay invested at 10 percent for ten years, it will be worth $2,207; at twenty years $7,330; at thirty years $19,842; and at forty years $53,715.

Let us take a break for a moment and use this opportunity to discuss the fact that the Torah forbids a Jew to loan money to a fellow Jew at interest; yet the Torah allows a Jew to take interest from a non-Jew. Question: If taking interest is unethical, why may we take interest from a non-Jew? This question has perplexed and frustrated many people.

However, it is beautifully explained by the *Torah Temimah*. I would like to introduce the explanation with a *mashal*, a parable.

There was a group of men who were lifelong friends. They grew up together, went to school together, and spent much time together. They genuinely liked each other and decided to create a bond of friendship. One of the ways they demonstrated this special bond was to allow members of their special "club" the use each others' cars at will. For example, if Mr. Ruben suddenly needed a car and his friend Shimon wasn't home, Mr. Ruben would go over to Shimon's house and "borrow" his car. The privilege of taking a car without even asking permission was a special favor they granted to each other as a sign of their unique friendship.

If a neighbor who was not a member of this special friendship club asked to take Shimon's car without permission, Shimon would say, "No way! That's a privilege granted only to our club members!"

That is how the *Torah Temimah* explains the reason a Jew may not charge a fellow Jew interest. Logically, just as you can charge money for the borrowing of a tool, lawnmower, or a car, you should be able to charge for the use of your money. But Hashem wanted the loaning of money to demonstrate the special bond of friendship among his children, the *Bnei Yisrael*. Thus the law of interest-free loans applies only to Jews.

Interestingly, the Gemara tells us that Hashem told *Bnei Yisrael* that He would take them out of Egypt only if they would commit to not taking interest from each other. Why is the commandment of not taking interest from a fellow Jew connected to the redemption from Egypt? Perhaps it is because the redemption was the moment when the Jews became a nation. It was the actual time of the "bonding" and therefore it was the perfect moment to command us about the special bond of friendship.

There is nothing intrinsically unethical about charging interest on a loan. Just as a person can charge rent for the use of a tool, in the same way he is entitled to charge interest for the use of his money. The Torah, however, forbade the taking of interest from a fellow Jew as a sign of this special friendship bond.

16.
ATTITUDE TOWARD MONEY
Part Four

*S*ince money is such an important part of our lives, I am attempting to develop a lesson plan whereby we can teach children some of the basic concepts of investing.

Here is an interesting thought: The young adult who was never taught about investing, never invested any money, and has no investment plan, is prey to any exciting "money making" scheme.

Just imagine a group of young men, each of whom has a few dollars from his bar mitzvah and summer work. One of the group suddenly comes upon a way to make lots of "real money," whether it be with a pork-belly commodity purchase, silver mine, dot com shares, or other get-rich schemes. Human nature being what it is, everyone wants to make money. A young man who knows nothing about investing money and who has no plan is ignorant and trusting, often becoming the unfortunate victim of a well-meaning but misguided venture.

I think parents should teach their children attitudes and behavior about investing, just as they do in all other areas of life. Parents do try to teach children how to limit their spending — and that is surely important — but learning how to invest money is equally important. Actually, the attitude children develop toward spending money will be put into better perspective when it is balanced with the ability to use the money saved and invest it.

Moreover, because the discussion of investing money is not confrontational — you are not saying to your child, "Don't spend money on this purchase" — it is more likely that you will be heard.

To date, we covered two negative concepts about money:
1. Inflation eats away savings.
2. Taxes take away about one-third of all earnings.

We also covered one positive concept:
3. The magic of compound interest helps.

We are now ready for the next lesson:
4. The magic of tax deferral helps, too.

If there is any subject prone to "information overload," it is a discussion of taxes. Because there are rules, by-laws, special cases, exceptions to the rules, exemptions, etc., and because the tax laws aren't a well-thought-out system but rather a hodgepodge of years of added laws offset by loopholes, they are truly confusing. The result is that most people turn off completely the minute the word "taxes" is mentioned.

At the risk of oversimplifying our discussion to the point of omitting some facts, I would like to present just one aspect of taxes.

As we mentioned, we pay about one-third of all money earned to the government. Therefore, if we put $1000 into a savings bank and earn $50, we have to pay $16 in taxes. The second year we have only $1034 to start off our investment.

What would happen if we could start the second year with the full $1050 and pay the taxes at some future date? Would there be an appreciable benefit if we could defer taxes to some future time and invest that money instead?

Using the magic of compounded interest — interest earning interest — the difference in twenty, thirty or forty years would be astounding. For example, $1000 invested at 12 percent with one-third of earnings paid to taxes every year would be worth over $90,000 in thirty years. The same $1000 with all earnings reinvested (no taxes paid) would be worth over $190,000 in thirty years.

The government does have such an arrangement, called "tax deferred," which simply means you push away the obligation to pay taxes now. In the simplest program you defer it to a later date. The government allows a person to put away $2,000 each year without paying taxes on the earnings until years later.

17.
ATTITUDE TOWARD MONEY
Part Five

*I*n the last chapter I discussed tax deferral. I would be remiss if I didn't point out the opportunity for you to discuss with your child two important points about this topic.

The first is our need to appreciate the United States of America for being a *malchus* of *chesed* — a benevolent government. During the late 1800's and early 1900's, America was the major (if not single) safe haven for hundreds of thousands of Jews who were running away from poverty, oppression, and brutality.

In the last few decades it has become fashionable to berate the government. Almost anyone can list a long litany of complaints against any branch of the government, be it local, state, or federal (or all three)! But as responsible parents I think it behooves us to make sure that our children first have a genuine appreciation for the kindness of America, for its unique freedom of religion, and for the opportunity it offers us as Jews. Never in the history of the world has any nation extended these privileges to Jews. We may complain about taxes, other government policies, and politics (and we may be right!), but we shouldn't let that get in the way of our appreciation.

These conversations also offer us the opportunity to speak about the Jews' special obligation to be scrupulously honest. Children sometimes develop a dichotomous mentality, thinking that mitzvos are to be done at home and in school, but that there are different rules in the marketplace, on Wall Street, and in the shopping malls. This is antithetical to our entire belief system. We shouldn't forget that the child may be most receptive to hearing *Chazal's* wisdom regarding appreciation and honesty at this moment.

Having said that, let's go back to this chapter's lesson, our fifth.

5. Mutual funds may be a wise investment. (If we haven't lost you yet with compound interest and taxes, you'll do just fine with mutual funds!)

A mutual fund simply means shares of many companies bought and managed by a team of experts. You can buy into these shares so that you have a diversity of many companies and industries, and experts who monitor the investment.

Owning shares of major companies has proven over the last hundred years to be a great investment if you …

a) diversify into numerous companies and industries, and

b) have an expert monitor the investments.

If you bought these shares at any time, even at the worst time, and kept them for a long while, you would have done exceptionally well.

How much can mutual funds earn? To cut through all the fancy talk, let us say that over the last fifty years in any period of eight years or longer the average return was over 10 percent per year.

There is a need to discuss the relation between risk and earnings. Money in a bank carries the least risk; mutual funds do carry a measure of risk. But when you talk "long term" ten, twenty, thirty, and more years, this risk — measured against the eating away of inflation — becomes small.

The concept of risk versus reward deserves a full discussion. It starts with a basic understanding that there are no free lunches, that you can't get anything of value for nothing. When you buy a lottery ticket, your potential for reward is very high — $10 million for the $1 ticket you bought! But your risk of losing is equally high — seven million to one. High risk; high reward.

The same basic concept underlies every investment. When the investment is really secure — as for example, when it is backed by the government — the earnings are small; 4, 5, or 6 percent a year. When you buy into a solid company with a little risk, the earnings could be 7 to 10 percent a year, but then there is some risk. If you buy into a company with a high risk and the company does well, you could earn 20 or 30 percent in one year ... but, on the other hand, the company could fail and you could lose your entire investment.

The real lesson here is that there is no sure thing with high earnings. A child (and many adults) has to be taught that the words "sure thing" and "make a lot of money" just don't go together. There are, of course, opportunities to make money, but you have to fully understand the risk factor. To do otherwise is foolhardy. Teach your child that if it sounds "too good to be true," it is!

18.

ATTITUDE TOWARD MONEY
Part Six

e are finally coming to the end of our discussion of investing, attempting to lay out a complex subject in a simple, easy-to-understand way. I have chosen investing as our topic because it is just the type of subject that often is not taught due to "information overload."

In the last chapter I introduced the concept of mutual funds, which are large pools of shares in different companies, managed by a team of experts.

Mutual funds make the most logical first investment for the following reasons:

a) We are investing for the long term — ten, twenty, thirty, or forty years.

b) It is easy to get started with this investment; many mutual funds will accept $100.

c) They will automatically reinvest all the earned money, so you will enjoy the benefits of compounding.

c) Hopefully, the team of experts will watch the fund.

d) The mutual fund will do all the paperwork, setting up the "tax-deferred" status.

There are two ways to start your investment in a mutual fund. Get an investment broker to select and watch one for you. He will take an up-front commission of up to 8 percent, which means if you give him $1000 to invest, he will invest only $920. Otherwise, be ready and willing to do the initial selection and watching yourself and purchase a no-commission fund.

The mutual funds that do not charge a commission are called "no-load" funds, as opposed to the funds that do charge sales commissions, which are called "load" funds. You can find advertisements for both in the financial sections of most newspapers.

Now let's see if we can compile some of the ideas we have been discussing.

a) Begin to use the magic of tax-deferred. The government calls this an IRA (or Keogh, or 401k); what it means is that you don't pay taxes now on money earned. When you will be 59 years old and want to use the money, you'll pay taxes on what you use. The difference in earnings between tax-deferred or regular taxed earnings is tremendous.

b) Start to invest early, when you are young, so the money will compound and have time to work its magic. (Two thousand dollars invested at age 18 at 10 percent a year compounded, is worth over $62,000 forty years later.) This figure may not seem very impressive, but realize that if an 18-year-old invested $1,000 (in an IRA at 10 percent a year) and did it again for only the next seven years — a total of $8,000 invested — when he is 65 years old it would be worth over $500,000!

c) Develop a plan to invest monthly (even if it is a small sum) to take advantage of "averaging" (called dollar-cost averaging), so it will make no difference if the market is up or down.

d) Consider balancing your investments between high-risk and low-risk investments.

The longer the time frame, the more "risk" you should be willing to take.

As in so many other projects, there is a risk that children will get carried away by the excitement of investing. The parent has to carefully adjust and monitors the interest level of each child to his or her specific needs.

∽◌∾

One last point. *Chazal* teach us that "Blessings only come to things that are hidden from the eye." Life experiences teach us that people who talk openly about their "great gains" usually don't tell us at all about their "great losses!"

Be wary of anyone who parades how smart he is in any area, but especially in finances.

19.

ATTITUDE TOWARD MONEY
Part Seven

n preparing for this section on "Attitudes Toward Money" I interviewed many people and discovered a tremendous interest in "the market."

I found it disturbing to meet men and women who are in various businesses, professions, or still in school, but who seem to be attached by phone or computer to the market.

These people grasp at a 5-minute break — lunchtime, driving from one place to another, a few minutes wait before a meeting, or during recess — to catch up on the market, or to make a trade.

With the availability of cell phones, 800 numbers, online trading and 24-hour trading, almost anyone can "be in the market" at any time, day or night.

If someone is a professional trader, he knows the industry, has done his research, and has paid his "*rebbe gelt*" (a Yiddish expression which simply means "paid the price to learn the business"), then buying and selling stocks is his business; it requires time, effort, and attention.

My following comments are addressed to those who are not Wall Street professionals, but who are engaged full time in some other field of endeavor. To watch such a person spend some time, a good portion of his mind, and a lot of his conversation in the market is distressing.

When you see a person "glued" to the market, you can be assured that in almost every case he has no well thought out investment plan, or no significant retirement program.

It is likely that just because he has no such plan he is desperately trying to "make a killing" in the market ... a sure-fire way to disaster.

First, study after study shows that people who buy stock on hot tips or as a reflex to the daily market almost always lose. Many times they get burned badly. Second, when a person's mind is in the market, he cannot give full concentration to the work at hand.

Moreover, it is this type of person who buys impulsively; the type who is prone to go in over his head — even to the point of borrowing money to invest — in a "sure thing."

Last, being attached to the market in this way does not promote a serenity to be able to devote time and mind to the more important things in life.

The objective of this series is clearly not to promote, encourage, or condone our "infatuation" with the market, or to be addicted to its daily fluctuations. To the contrary, our goal is to have a program to make monthly investments, periodically check on them, and beyond that to enjoy the peace of mind of "planned abandonment."

As we complete this series let us review the *hashkafah* lessons this subject has offered:

a) All wealth belongs to Hashem.

b) It is important to allocate a *tzedakah* fund.

c) It is important to save for the future.

d) Saving develops self-discipline.

e) It is important to know the laws of *ribbis* (interest).

f) A Jew has a special obligation to be scrupulously honest.

g) A Jew has an obligation toward the government.

h) Hashem's blessing comes only when things are kept private.

Hopefully these selected ideas will spur fuller discussions between you and your children about money.

20.

ASSUMPTIONS

*A*s an addendum to the previous chapters on attitudes toward investing, I feel it important to discuss the concept of assumptions.

The suggestions offered, especially regarding mutual funds, are based on the assumption that the economy continues as it has in the last fifty years, with investors enjoying a more-than-10 percent return a year. But no one knows for sure if this will continue over the next decades, and it would be misleading if I gave our readers any suggestion to the contrary. In every area of life, especially in finance, we live with assumptions, and we have reason to believe, to assume, that these are good investments, but we have no guarantees.

In management courses we are taught, "Assumptions are the mother of all foul-ups." I remember a student telling me that his professor made the class repeat this sentence tens of times until it became a natural reflex: The moment you hear a problem, you think that "problems are caused by assumptions," and you try to identify the wrong assumption. What this means in simple language is that when we examine what went wrong in a project, we usually find that we had assumed something that we later found out was not true. The advice presented in the pithy aphorism "Assumptions are the mother of all foul-ups" is that if we were to check out all assumptions, we would reduce a major cause of problems.

We live with assumptions. When you drive through a green light at an intersection, you are assuming that cars who have a red light will stop. When you drive down a main street, you assume that cars coming to the stop sign at the corner of the side street will all stop.

In *halachah* we have the term *chazakah*, which means that we take something for granted based on previous experience. Thus, if we know a *mikveh* had adequate water yesterday, we don't have to measure it today before we *toivel* a dish. Unless we have reason to suspect differently, we can assume that if it was kosher yesterday, it is still kosher today.

Yet there are exceptions to the laws of *chazakah*, and one exception is the concept of an easily checked *chazakah*. For example, the *halachah* suggests that a man quickly check his *tzitzis* every morning before he puts them on because it is such an easy thing to do. Where does this leave us with regard to our discussion of investments? On one hand, we live by assumptions; on the other hand, assumptions cause our major problems. On one hand, in order to protect what we have from inflation and to enjoy the benefits of compounding interests, we need to invest our money; on the other hand, no investment is foolproof or even guaranteed. The answer lies somewhere in the middle ground.

We have to teach our children (and ourselves) that we must challenge and think through assumptions. We have to ask and question to the best of our ability. Simultaneously, we have to move ahead and take calculated risks.

If we always rely blindly on assumptions, we will be disappointed; if we never take risks, we will be paralyzed into non-action.

We're talking about investing money … but we are really talking about much more. We are talking about life itself.

A child has to be trained to recognize assumptions and risks, and to develop a smart working policy on how to manage them. Perhaps working with a child on his investments is a good way to teach him this balancing act for all areas of life.

21.
A LETTER

Dear Mr. Shulman,

I greatly enjoy your articles and books because they open new areas of thought and stimulate family discussion. You have taught me to mull over, reflect, and muse on an idea.

I recently read a statement that set my mind going, and I would like to share it with you. The sentence read, "Our attitudes are the outward expressions of our belief." I think what the author is trying to say is that a person can declare his belief in any way he wants to — by talking about it, by writing, by making speeches … but in actuality, his attitudes are the true expressions of his beliefs.

If I understand this correctly, then our beliefs and attitudes have to be in synch, in line with each other, and if not, it means our beliefs are not what we say they are.

I have taken the liberty to expand on this theme and have sent my ideas to you. If you are comfortable with them and if you want to share them with your readers, I would be honored.

Our attitudes are the outward expressions of our belief.

If we believe that we are in the hands of Hashem ... our attitude toward problems should be confidence and serenity.

If we believe that we are Hashem's nation ... our attitude toward our religion should be pride and responsibility.

If we believe that only Torah and mitzvos are eternal ... our attitude toward materialism should be that it is insignificant.

If we believe that a shul is a miniature Beis HaMikdash ... our attitude toward it should be reverence and respect.

If we believe that our prayers can open the reservoir of blessings ... then our attitude toward them should be attentiveness, and they should be heartfelt.

If we believe that our children's learning is our important concern ... our attitude toward an appeal would be appreciation.

If we believe that learning Torah is our single most important mitzvah ... our attitude toward learning would be eager involvement.

If we believe that improving our middos is a major purpose of our life ... our attitude toward anyone who criticizes us would be thankfulness.

I hope you enjoy these.

Very truly yours,
A loyal reader

22.

UNLIMITED FUNDING

was employed by a correspondence school that taught a course in tax preparation. The company was owned by a *ben Torah* and was operated on the highest level of ethical principles. The sales brochures represented the offer honestly, the students were treated attentively, and those students who completed the course of study with passing grades had a good grasp of tax preparations for the individual.

One day the owner decided to apply for admission to a quasi-official home-study council that advertised nationally and represented seventy or eighty various correspondence schools. To qualify for admission we had to go through an elaborate procedure that included answering fifty questions in minute detail. These questions were presented to us in an official document, and when the answers to these questions were completed, the finished product was a nearly one-hundred-page "book," of which fifteen copies had to be submitted.

Most of the questions dealt with the procedures of admissions, pricing, quality, suitability, and updates of the text, qualifications of the instructors, etc. All questions were smart and appropriate.

The last question was a stickler. It read, "If your organization had unlimited funding, list all the ideas that you could institute to improve in each area of your service." We struggled with the answers to that question for hours and finally came up with twenty ideas.

After the fifteen "books" were sent to the council, a team of investigators came to visit us to discuss the answers we submitted. During the interview I asked, "What was the purpose of the last question, since I have never known of an organization that had unlimited funding? Weren't the answers to this question just an act of futility, playing out an imaginary but non-existing situation?"

The head of the delegation was the owner of one of the largest, most successful participating schools, a man who had spent a lifetime in this industry. He looked at me intently and told me that in all his years he had found that most people have tremendously creative ideas, but unfortunately they don't allow themselves to think creatively because "they can't afford it." He went on to explain that since many new ideas require some investment of money, and since money is usually unavailable for these new ideas, people tend not even to allow themselves to think of any new ideas. The richest source of bright new ideas is choked off even before it gets a chance! To get around this problem the delegate concluded, he had found the need to set aside the problem of not having enough money, and then the creative juices would begin to flow.

There is an interesting ending to this story. After we had listed twenty ideas that could improve our service, we found that several of them could be done at little or no additional expense! This discovery highlighted the double lock we had placed on our creative thinking. We had restricted ourselves from coming up with ideas that did need investment, and in the process held back ideas that could be implemented *without* new funds.

Imagining what we would do with unlimited funds acts as a jolt to the thinking process.

Try it; you may be delighted with the results.

23.

DREAMS

here is often a moment in a relationship when you may notice a subtle change in attitude, an ever so slight movement from one position to another.

An example is in the dating process when the language used by the boy and girl changes from "I", "he," or "she" to "we."

In the selling process, it is when the prospective customer takes off a loose thread or some dust from the merchandise and asks how quickly it can be delivered ... a sign that he is beginning to view the item as his.

In the classroom, the experienced teacher can sense this moment when the students' eyes light up, as if to say, "Now we understand it!"

Some years ago I taught a small group of men a course on public speaking, goal setting, and time management.

After the fourth session, I sensed a changed attitude in the group. They were more relaxed, more trusting and open.

The eighth session was dedicated to goal setting, and the assignment was for each student to consider what he really would do with his life and to share this dream with us.

The problem with this type of assignment is that we don't allow ourselves the luxury of unrestricted creative thinking. Before we even begin to develop the idea, we immediately torpedo it with a negative thought. For example, if a person wanted to think about opening a certain type of business, even before entertaining the notion he would counter it with the mental comment, "I don't have the money it takes …" His dream would come to an immediate dead end.

You can't do much creative thinking if at the same time you are "realistic" and allow the negative thought to cancel all the positive ones. This is similar to trying to drive a car with your right foot on the accelerator and your left foot on the brake. It just doesn't work.

To get around this problem and to encourage the students in my class to really think "big," I created an imaginary *malach* who would take care of all logistical and financial problems. Now, with no problems, how "big" would they think? In the motivational field, the question is, "What great things would you do if you were guaranteed success?"

At that session I witnessed a phenomenon. All the participants outlined plans to accomplish worthwhile projects.

But there were two students especially who allowed their imaginations to soar. They each had specific outlines of what they wanted to do, and they spoke with great passion and enthusiasm. They had done much private thinking, recognized a need, identified how this need could be filled, and presented a step-by-step outline of how the project could be accomplished.

The fascinating thing is that within two years, both men had begun these projects — one a school and the other a *chesed* program — and to this day these projects are flourishing.

24.

"SHARING IDEAS"

*I*n the last chapter I wrote of two young men who who had taken a course I gave in goal setting. Both had laid out major programs that in the next few years they saw to fruition.

I noted with interest that both of these young men — as with others in the group — had never discussed these dreams with anyone!

My question to them was, "Why didn't you discuss your dreams with other people?" Both of them answered almost verbatim, "Because we didn't want to be put down!"

An idea is very personal and fragile. It represents the person's thinking, and often his ego can't handle the sarcasm, put-downs and verbal abuse, albeit well-meaning, routinely dished out by friends.

Just imagine this scenario: A group of friends is at the breakfast table, a *kiddush*, or *sheva berachos* and you casually mention that you're planning to write a book, or become the vice president of a company, or become a councilman in your community. In all probability, your friends' reactions would be somewhere in the neighborhood of, "You, write a book? You can't even write two sentences in English!" or, "What did you eat last night that gave you this bad dream?" or some other deprecating comment.

Since most people can't handle such negative talk, the person who does have this ambition would probably choose not to present it to his friends.

Perhaps negative, snide, and sarcastic put-downs have become a way of life as a result of decades of sitcom programs, where this type of talk is usual. Perhaps it is the result of our eroding respect for elders and for people in general. Whatever the reason, the end result is a society where deprecation is the norm, and support and encouragement are exceptions.

It then occurred to me that because in our small class we didn't allow any negative talk, there was no need for the students to hide their goals. On the contrary, the student who said he wanted to do something spectacular would in all likeliood get the following response: "Great! Let's make a list of what skills you will need to do exactly what you want to do!"

The principle here is that in nearly all cases — and there are few exceptions — people can really do great things if — and this is the key word — if they are ready to pay the price by acquiring the talents and skills needed and developing these to a professional level.

Most people tend to play the devil's advocate much too early and much too strongly in the development stage of an idea, without providing the balance of support and nurturance. Often we need more "angel" and less "devil."

Yes, it is extremely important to get the input of friends in the development of an idea. But be careful to share your idea with and to ask advice from positive, supportive people.

25.
LIVING FOREVER
Part One

Rabbi Yaakov Kamenetsky *zt"l* once explained why a person behaves as though he will live forever, when in reality every person knows that life is finite.

When the Almighty created man, His intent was that man live forever. Only after Adam sinned was man doomed to die. However, since man was originally destined to live forever, the fabric of his being — his spiritual DNA, so to speak — is programmed for eternal life. The result is that he does not view death as a reality. We know intelligently that it happens, we even acknowledge the fact that we knew people who have died ... but nevertheless, we do not live as though it is a reality.

There are two specific concerns that are circumvented by the "living forever" syndrome. The first is writing a will, the second is buying *karka* (a grave site). Neither subject is pleasant to discuss, but is nevertheless important.

Writing a will is a privilege granted by the state for the distribution of money and property according to the desire of the owner. Without a will, a whole group of complex laws goes into effect, some of which may be diametrically opposed to the desire of the person who died. Who will inherit which property and who will provide for whom are questions that, when no official will has been provided, will be answered by the state, to the satisfaction of a judge. Thus, a judge appointed trustee may make the decision as to whether or not an orthodontist bill is more important than special tutoring for a child.

You would be hard pressed to imagine all the comedic and tragic scenarios that take place when an outsider is given the authority to distribute someone's estate. Heartbreak that can last decades and permanently divide families can so easily be avoided when we're able to face the great reality of life — that at some time everyone will die.

Somehow we believe that, just as we won't catch a contagious disease if we don't come near the person who has it, so too we won't "catch death" if we don't discuss it.

The Chofetz Chaim writes that people live as though there is a "special club whose members die" … and they choose not to join that club.

Writing a will requires much thought. Provisions for a spouse and children have to be considered, disposal of property has to be carefully weighed. There are also many halachic issues that have to be thought through and which can be resolved with planning.

Because a will can be changed and rewritten, you don't have to be concerned about how to leave your estate years from now. You only have to consider how to leave your estate now and in the next few years.

Chazal tell us that for the first 2300 years after Creation, when it was time for a person to die, death came suddenly, without a warning. It was Yaakov Avinu who asked Hashem to give people notice of impending death and thus, as a favor to man, sickness as a precursor to death was created.

Rabbi Pam, in a *Chumash shiur* on *Parshas Vayechi,* explained the *chesed* of being given an opportunity to remove oneself from the hustle and bustle of everyday life to put his spiritual and financial "house" in order. Not everyone is given this opportunity. We all know of young men and women who died suddenly. Since making a will is a relatively simple process, it makes good sense to do so immediately.

26.

LIVING FOREVER
Part Two

*I*n the last chapter I discussed the *chesed* that the Almighty did to Yaakov Avinu by giving notice to people of impending death. As a result, sickness as a precursor to death was created. This column addresses the advantages of writing a will.

Some things to take into consideration when making a will:

1. Children can view an inheritance as an expression of their parent's love for them. Thus, if a person has three children, two of whom are financially independent and one of whom is poor, the parent may want to leave a larger portion of his estate to the poor child. He is advised to

give careful thought to the implied message that the other children may read into such a division. "Father (or Mother) loves the third child more than he loves us." A parent may be advised to give money to the third child while the parent is still alive, create a special fund for him, or provide a special insurance policy for him, but all of these are "outside of the inheritance" and thus not a measure of the parent's love. The "inheritance" can then remain equal for all the children.

2. There are two well-known *halachos* regarding an estate: a) If the firstborn is a son, he inherits an extra portion (called *pi shenayim*). b) Sons, but not daughters, inherit a father's estate. The rabbis realized years ago that there are practical situations when these *halachos* have to be circumvented, and they have provided halachic formulas to do this. It is important to consult with an authority in Torah estate laws before going to an attorney to draw up a will. As with everything else in life, you have to know what you are doing. Getting proper information makes it easy.

3. Consider writing an "ethical will." An ethical will expresses the parent's desire about how children should behave. *Chazal* tell us, and our own observation verifies this point, that the words of a person before he dies — his admonitions, advice, guidance — are powerful messages remembered for decades. Moreover, wise words at this

time will be very comforting for the family. Not every person merits the time, preparation, and clarity of mind before death to deliver a meaningful ethical will. Wise people have prepared such a document while they can think clearly, without undue emotion. The document can be put away, together with the will, to be opened "after 120 years." Like the will, it should be reviewed every few years to make sure that it reflects the current, up to date needs of the family.

4. You may want to allocate *tzedakah* to various causes for your own *zchus*. We would hope that children and others will give the appropriate share of *tzedakah* from the inheritance, but that is their mitzvah. I am talking about the *niftar's tzedakah*. Also, the specific charities to receive the donations and even the amounts could be spelled out to insure that your wishes are fulfilled.

It should be pointed out that your "charity list" should be reviewed every few years to be sure that the organizations you have listed still deserve your *tzedakah*. There have been situations where people wrote a *tzedakah* list attached to their will, and when they died decades later their families discovered that a synagogue mentioned is no longer Orthodox or an organization listed no longer has the same objectives. It hurts to imagine that part of the *niftar's* estate is donated to a cause he would not at this time want to support.

27.
LIVING FOREVER
Part Three

In the last chapter I began a discussion of a difficult topic — facing up to the reality that no one lives forever. I discussed writing a legal will and preparing an ethical will. Now, I'd like to discuss buying *karka* (burial ground) and leaving clear instructions for whatever arrangements are to be made after a person's passing.

I think it only appropriate to begin this discussion by telling you that there is a merit for living a long life in buying *karka* before it is needed.

Buying a grave site is an emotionally draining decision for anyone to make. It is difficult enough for an adult to make this decision in good health, with a clear head, in a positive frame of mind. Imagine how much more difficult it becomes if such a decision has to be made when the person is sick (it can be misunderstood as foretelling impending death) or when he is depressed.

If this decision is left to be made by a grieving spouse or children at the parent's deathbed, a difficulty has been compounded into a traumatic, gut-wrenching experience. Moreover, when no clear instructions have been given, the question as to where to bury a spouse or a parent, or how to make other funeral arrangements, can develop into arguments that can divide a family. To force children to make such a decision under the worst circumstances is unfair and thoughtless.

A person who faces this eventuality with intelligent honesty would do the following:

a) He would decide on where he is to be buried. Sometimes this decision is obvious, but with the advent of burial possibilities in Israel, this question is not simple at all.

b) He should purchase and fully pay for the plot. I have reason to believe that there is a difference in price when a grave site is bought for future use and when it is bought for immediate need. Second, at the actual time of *petirah*, the family finances may be stretched to the limit because of illness or other reasons. When the burial plot is paid for, it is one less headache for the family. Moreover, it is an expression of concern for the surviving family members.

c) Become a member and support a *Chevrah Kaddisha* (an Orthodox burial society). In a community where there are several *Chevrei Kaddisha* this choice becomes very important.

d) He should perhaps purchase adjoining plots for other members of the family.

e) He should write instructions as to what should or should not be done at the funeral.

f) He should write instructions as to the *Kaddish*, learning of Mishnayos, *yahrzeit*, etc. If a person does not convey such instructions, the family will be left to do what they imagine the *niftar* wanted, sometime rightly or sometime wrongly. The danger here is the opportunity for children to disagree as to what they imagine a parent would have wanted.

Rav Pam told a number of stories of great men who left *tzavaos* — instructions — as to their funerals. While details vary from story to story, the thread that winds through all these stories is a mature, open approach to the subject.

The purpose of these few lines is not to upset the reader, but rather to provoke him or her to take action now, write a will now ... and then live many years with peace of mind, knowing he is prepared.

28.
HONORING PARENTS
Part One

*Y*ou come home from a two-day trip. The children are sitting at the dining room table after supper, doing their homework. You walk into the dining room and say, "Hello."

Do your children stand up for you? Do you want your children to stand up, or do you feel that expecting them to stand up is such an uncomfortable request that you opt to pardon and dismiss it?

The *halachos* honoring parents are quite clear. Included in this mitzvah are rising upon seeing one's parents, cheerfully providing for one's parents with their needs, helping them dress, escorting them, and various other tasks.

Therefore, in strict compliance with the law, as children are taught to perform every other mitzvah — wear *tzitzis*, read *Krias Shema*, reciting *berachos* — in the very same way, they should be taught to stand up when a father or mother comes back home.

There is, however, an exemption from this law: The *halachah* states that parents may grant permission to a child in their home not to rise when they enter.

So here we have an interesting situation. On one hand, we have a law that is of such significance that there are commentaries which consider it Biblical in origin. The Torah equates giving honor to parents with giving honor to the Almighty. On the other hand, parents are allowed to waive the fulfillment of this obligation — and in our liberal society it is so much easier to forgo this demand, inasmuch as many parents would be uncomfortable or even embarrassed to ask a child to rise when they walk into the house.

What does a parent do?

Before we discuss this question, we should know the facts about the *halachah* of rising for a parent.

The *halachah* applies when both parent and child are in the same room or area; thus, a child on a different floor of the same building as a parent need not rise, although he sees and hears the parent enter. Likewise, a girl sitting in the woman's section of a synagogue who sees her father entering the men's section does not have to rise.

How often does a child have to rise in honor of parents? There are basic differences between Sephardic and Ashkenazic customs. The Sephardic custom is for a child to rise every time a parent enters or reenters a room, regardless of how many times a day this happens.

The Ashkenazic practice, according to many commentaries, limits the obligation to rise in honor of a parent to once in the morning and once at night. However, if people are present who are unaware that a child had risen earlier, the child is obligated to rise for the parent again.

In practical terms, our question is this: A father or mother comes home at night and the children are sitting on the floor or around the the table playing. Do the parents insist that the children stand for them, or do they release the children from this mitzvah?

29.

HONORING PARENTS
Part Two

*I*n the last chapter I asked the question: If a parent comes home at night and his children are sitting on the floor playing or doing their homework at the dining room table, does he want the children to stand up for him as an expression of honor, or does he automatically release them from this mitzvah?

Granted that the parent has the right to release his children from the mitzvah — but is this wise? Since this practice can teach young children the importance of respect, is it smart to forgo the lesson because we find it awkward?

When I asked couples how they actively teach their children to respect and fear them, I received many puzzled looks and a lot of interesting answers.

There were couples who told me that parents today need to offer friendship and "camaraderie" to their children, not to instill respect and fear. The overriding need is for children to trust parents, and with the challenges of the teen years, their trust should be fostered at all cost. Since the *halachah* allows parents to waive this mitzvah, why insist on fear and respect when they can create a barrier between parent and child?

There were other parents who told me that they did not allow the children to sit on the father's or mother's seat at the Shabbos table, did not allow them to begin eating until the father began, and did not allow them to walk through the front door before the parents when coming home on Shabbos.

Here is an interesting thought. Perhaps, fifty or sixty years ago, parents may have felt that requiring a child to rise when they come home was out of sync with Western society, and therefore they took advantage of the halachic allowance to waive this obligation. But today we live in a time when *derech eretz* (respect for others) is at an all time low.

All around us we hear complaints that children don't have respect. Parents confront school principals, *rebbeim*, and *moros* with this complaint; and *rebbeim* and *moros* have the identical complaint against parents. Perhaps in this context, the mitzvah to respect parents takes on an additional dimension.

In a small booklet published by D.E.R.E.C.H., entitled "Producing Loveable Children," Mrs. S.C. Radcliffe writes a few paragraphs that I want to share with you.

"It is a mitzvah to rise for one's parents.

"A common reaction is to shun this precept as archaic. Before passing judgment, however, it behooves us as Jewish parents to examine the mitzvah in depth.

"Perhaps the most obvious way of demonstrating honor is to rise for a person. After all, who is it that we stand up for in our lives? We all stand up for judges; we all stand up for the president or prime minister; and we stand up for our great rabbis and Torah teachers. Standing up is a sign of honor.

"Unfortunately, the mitzvah of standing up for one's parents (twice a day) presents a major challenge to parents living in a democratic milieu. We are not accustomed to seeing people rise for their parents anymore — although this was once common behavior. In truth, rising is probably more important today than it ever was; in a generation characterized by *chutzpah yisgei*, prevalent brazenness, one must bend over backwards to get to the middle road. Indeed, the Rambam advises that in order to correct flaws in character, a person should go to the other extreme."

30.
HONORING PARENTS
Part Three

n the last chapter I began a quote from the D.E.R.E.C.H. booklet entitled, "Producing Loveable Children," on the topic of respect for parents.

There are two additional points presented.

"There is another reason why rising for parents is important. In democratic-style parenting, children are actually robbed of the security of adult protection and guidance because parents and children are considered to be 'peers.' Children who rise for their parents, on the other hand, are protected by this mitzvah because it preserves essential boundaries; the result is security for the child who recognizes adult status and authority. Although Judaism views parents and children to be of equal worth and value, they are seen as having different positions in the world: Parents are to serve as guides and teachers, while children are seen as students of life. The establishment and protection of boundaries in the parent-child relationship feels right and good to children.

"Finally, this mitzvah is particularly powerful in its ability to instill humility, honor, and reverence in the child. When a child stands up twice a day for his parents, he not only displays this honor, but he also comes to experience it — respect becomes an integral part of his psyche. Major breaches of respect are much less likely to occur in a youngster whose daily habit is to show honor in this way.

"Similarly, it is much less likely that a child will grow into a verbally abusive adolescent (one who defies and/or insults his parents) when that child has been trained in the precept of rising. Honoring parents by rising for them is simply incompatible with gross disrespect. Those who grow up with the mitzvah of rising for parents find the act easy and natural to perform."

❧

While these chapters deal primarily with the one *halachah* of rising for a parent, I don't mean to ignore the other *halachos* by which a child expresses respect and fear for a parent: not sitting in their special seat; not calling father or mother by name; not interrupting or correcting them, etc.

I have chosen to discuss the issue of rising for a parent because when a child does so, it pronouncedly and noticeably expresses respect. Many of the other laws are not as conspicuous to the casual observer.

31.
HONORING PARENTS
Part Four

*I*n the last three chapters I discussed honoring parents. I'd like to share a letter, with permission of the author, but have purposely omitted the author's name so you can judge it on its own merit.

Modern parenting fails. It fails at producing caring, giving, self-sacrificing human beings — the kind of human beings the world depends upon for working on great causes and moving us forward. Hard work, duty, obligation — these words do not exist in the modern vocabulary. Indeed they represent the antithesis of current values, which stress fun, self-fulfillment, and instant gratification. Today's children know how to get what they want. What they don't know is how to give others what they need.

And it is our fault. We have misled them. From the time they were infants, we worked hard to give them everything, to gratify their every need and wish. Past toddlerhood, when the first stirrings of independent striving occur, we did for them and did some more. Into the school years and into the teen years, our only concern was to make them happy and provide them with every opportunity, gift, and service that would enable them to flourish and prosper. Not that it was so wrong of us to give in this way. What was wrong was that we did not, in our process of diligent giving, teach them to give back — nor even to show gratitude!

The result is the "me" generation or, in heimish circles, the "es kumt mir" generation. This is a generation of children who feel that they are entitled to every good thing. When denied, their self-righteous anger knows no bounds. As young adults they are still demanding of their parents: "You owe me. Your money is mine. Buy me. Give me." Where did children ever learn the idea that the world exists for them? From their parents. We taught them this by our endless giving, never asking for anything in return, never teaching them that, in fact, it is we who are owed and not they.

Yes, children owe their parents — they owe them gratitude for bringing them into this world and for providing for them, taking care of them, educating them, and raising them to adulthood. They owe them honor and respect for being their teachers and leaders, their spiritual, emotional, and physical protectors, defenders, and guides. They owe them service in return for all the service that was provided. And if children can't recognize that they do, in fact, owe all of this to their parents — and more — then how will they recognize the good that anyone does for them — even Hashem? How will they develop the feeling of wanting to give in return? Indeed, instead of wanting to do for their children what their parents did for them, children like these are more likely to see their own offspring as impediments to their freedom and enjoyment of life! People who have been taught only to take and never to give find it difficult and cumbersome to give, give up, or to put themselves out.

Are these the children who will gladly bring their aging parents into their homes to return the caring and giving they once received? No. These children know little about serving Hashem, with putting their own interests aside. These children, used to having it all their way, cannot extend themselves beyond their comfort zones.

32.

HONORING PARENTS
Part Five

*I*n the last chapter I quoted from a letter. I want to continue with the same letter, which goes on to discuss a possible solution.

What can we do? Parenting must take a new direction. An old direction, really. Parenting must once again take on the shape and form of Torah. Torah parenting demands that a child learn, from his earliest years, to give. The commandment to honor our parents is laden with responsibilities of the child toward his parents. Hashem, knowing the loving heart he instilled within parents, does not command us to do for our children. He knows that we cannot help our-

selves — we will do everything we can do. However, in His wisdom, Hashem knows that children do not automatically feel the desire to do for others, not even their parents. This must be trained and instilled in them. Therefore He commands children to do for their parents. This mitzvah, this obligation, benefits only the child; through giving, the child comes to feel the sort of love for his parents that his parents feel naturally toward him. Love is generated by the very act of giving (Rav Dessler, "Strive for Truth"). It is up to parents to see to it that children learn to fulfill this mitzvah.

If we will teach our children to accept responsibilities toward us, they will learn that the world is not a "free ride." We must repay those who do good for us. Indeed, "the wicked one borrows and does not repay" (Avos 2:14). We must fulfill our own missions by putting out rather than by taking in. We are to be givers rather than takers — we are to produce, not passively receive. In this way, we become dynamic achievers, people who can offer the world something rather than demand their due from it.

Parents need a new (old) map in parenting in order to achieve the goal of raising children capable of such giving. We have been told enough how to raise our children's self-esteem. So much, in fact, that all our children have is self-esteem. Now, we must teach them how to have self-esteem for others by thinking about the feelings, needs, and wishes of others and striving to fulfill them. We must raise them with the yoke of giving, of taking of responsibility, so that this will be the only way for them to live. As soon as the child can talk, he must learn to say "thank you." As soon as he can walk, he must learn to bring his parents what they need. We cannot wait until the child is a teenager to begin to make demands upon him, for then it is far too late. He has already learned by that time that we are there to serve him, and not the other way around. No, we parents must start these lessons early and persevere throughout the parenting process.

Can it be done? Can we really raise children in today's world who will be comfortable with fulfilling their duties to man and to G-d? Yes. But we must support each other. Books, articles, parenting courses — all must move away from the philosophy of endless giving and begin to address the need of the parent to TEACH giving in accordance with Torah values. Then, with G-d's help, we will raise a new generation of children faithful to the values of their forefathers and ready to change today's world.

❦

Strong words! But what would your suggestions be?

33.
HONORING PARENTS
Part Six

e have been discussing the mitzvah of respecting and honoring one's parents, and the reasons to teach this to our children. Now I would like to address the larger question:

"How do we teach such a mitzvah?"

There is a short and long answer. This chapter will discuss the short answer. The next chapter will be dedicated to the long answer.

Many years ago a few couples asked me to give them a parenting course. We met for one night a week for eight weeks and had some fascinating discussions.

At one session the following question was raised:

"Is it right for you to use a mitzvah in such a way that it could be perceived that you are doing it for your own benefit?" Example: Parents sleeping on Shabbos afternoon are awakened by the noise made by their children. Is it right to say to the children, "Where is your observance of *kibud av v'aim?*"

We discussed the question for awhile, and I decided to ask Harav Yaakov Kamenetsky *zt"l*. A few days later I had the pleasure of speaking to the *Rosh Yeshiva*, who patiently listened to my question and then said, "The father should demand that the children play quietly to honor the mother, and when the opportunity arises, the mother should demand that the children do likewise to honor the father."

Many parents feel awkward about asking their children to stand up for them because the parent sees this as a request for his own honor. But in truth, while the child is standing up for you, he is really doing this for Hashem.

The parent should view himself as a minister appointed by the king. By respecting the minister, the citizen is actually showing respect to the king. In the same way, when the child respects or fears the parent, he is showing respect for Hashem.

A *rebbe* whom I have known for over four decades was "drafted" to become the rav of a local *shul*. He is one of the most humble men I know, and his modesty did not allow him to accept this position. It was only through the intervention of a *gadol* that he finally acquiesced and became rav. Having accepted this position, he now insists that his congregation give him the honor due to the office of the rav. For him to waive his *kavod* would be a disservice to the office.

Similarly, even if a parent feels inadequate, he has to believe that he is insisting upon respect for his station in life.

Obviously, the parents, like the rabbi, have to act like people who deserve to be respected. If a parent reduces himself to behaving in a demeaning or a shameful way, he can't expect children to respect him.

Once a parent believes that the children display respect for his station in life, he will become comfortable with this role.

34.
HONORING PARENTS
Part Seven

*I*n discussing the mitzvah with many people, it occurred to me that we learn about honoring parents differently than the way we learn most other mitzvos.

Several decades ago, when I began to listen seriously to speakers who lectured about parenting issues, I noticed to my chagrin that almost every speaker stated, as the first and foremost lesson: "You are the role model for your child. Therefore, do what's right, and the child will learn to do the same!"

I heard that advice so many times, in so many different ways, that I promised myself that if and when I ever speak to parents, I will offer that advice sparingly. Saying what we all know is true doesn't help much unless we also offer some practical guidance on how to make it happen.

That children learn by watching their parents is a given. It is a truism. But many times the impression made by the parents is balanced or offset by what others do. For example, a young child watches his father *daven* in *shul*, but he also observes the behavior of other people in *shul*. A young girl learns to make *berachos* by watching her mother, but again, this is offset by the fact that she will practice how to make *berachos* under the careful eye of a teacher.

In contrast to this, the mitzvah of honoring and respecting parents is primarily an in-house mitzvah. I think that it is fair to say that the vast majority of a young boy's or girl's attitude toward respecting parents is created by what happens in the privacy of their house, primarily by how the youngsters' parents relate to their own parents and in-laws. While teachers can teach the laws of how to honor parents, the classroom cannot offer many practical opportunities to practice these laws. Therefore, it is a subject that is almost entirely practiced at home, and what parents do becomes of primary importance.

I have discussed this issue with many people and have become aware of the many ways in which mature people show respect to their parents. There is a friend who takes off one whole day a week to visit and assist his aged parents in shopping; families who add extensions to their homes so they can provide a comfortable apartment for older parents; a friend who wrote a letter every week to his in-laws from the time he was married until they passed away (over fifteen years); a friend who would stand as a sign of respect whenever he spoke to either parent on the phone; a friend who would wear his Shabbos clothing when he called his mother. These are only a few examples of thousands of similar acts of private, in-house demonstrations of respect.

When we were youngsters, we thought the mitzvah of honoring and respecting parents consisted of listening to them when we were told to do something, such as finishing our cereal or wearing a sweater. As we mature and as our parents grow older, the focus of the mitzvah changes — visiting them, calling them, writing to them, taking them shopping, including them in our everyday life. These activities become the way we honor and respect our parents.

35.
BROAD STROKES
Part One

*I*f there is a fly on the table and you want to destroy it, what are your options? You can roll up a newspaper and swat it; you can use a book to hit it; you can use a sledgehammer; or you can use a fly swatter. In each case, if you hit the fly, you will kill it.

The difference in each of these four methods is not what happens to the fly, but rather what happens to the crystal glassware, the table setting, or the table itself. Using a rolled up newspaper, you risk breaking some dishes and crystal; using a book, you can cause the glasses to topple; using a sledgehammer, you will probably scratch or break the table. The fly swatter can best do the job without harming anything else.

This mundane observation has an important lesson for us.

Western culture implies that in almost every case "more and bigger are better." That's why wealthy people drive bigger cars and live in larger houses than they need, because they mistakenly reason that if they can afford it, why not? Isn't bigger always better?

There are many areas in life where less is more effective. For example, where criticism and punishment are concerned, most of the time less is better.

The thrust of this chapter is to discuss the effectiveness of words.

I have a friend who uses sweeping words, phrases, and statements. I first noticed this when he was driving and a small leaf was stuck to the windshield. His comment: "The leaf is driving me crazy." When I registered surprise at such strong language, he said what he meant was that the leaf was "annoying" him, and then he added, "But what's the difference? It's only words!"

Just as an intelligent craftsman uses the appropriate tool or instrument to do the right job, so too the intelligent person uses the right words to describe his feelings accurately. Words are the tools of the mind, the instruments with which we express our thoughts. To a large extent, the words we use create our frame of mind, our attitude.

As an example, when we use very strong words to express a relatively minor discomfort, we increase the discomfort.

"It's so cold I am freezing to death; it's so hot I'm boiling; if I don't make this sale, I'll go bankrupt!" We actually increase our own level of discomfort by the strong words we use!

Why is this so? Because our minds and our subconscious hear every word we speak, and they instruct the body to respond accordingly.

In contrast, we know people who have taught themselves to use language intentionally to reduce the level of discomfort. They might use words such as unpleasant, displease, disagree, unappealing, and distasteful to describe situations that others might describe as terrible, horrible, and tragic. The result of mild language is that it doesn't bring out the deep, negative emotions that strong words do.

When a milder, more gentle word will adequately convey your message, use it. Your mind will hear these words, and your body will react accordingly. More dramatic words don't do a better job. On the contrary, "broad strokes" in language may cause undesirable damage, like a sledgehammer.

We'll continue this thought in the next chapter.

36.
BROAD STROKES
Part Two

*I*n the last chapter I discussed what happens when a person uses "broad strokes" in language, words that overstate a situation. As an example, by using strong words to describe minor discomforts, we exacerbate the problem and actually increase our level of discomfort. Our mind and body "hear" the strong words and act accordingly.

Another very different facet to this topic is credibility.

Whenever a salesman tries to convince us to purchase a product or service, he may be tempted to exaggerate. If the speed of a printing press is an important factor, he may be tempted to "round off" the average speed from 7,000 to 9,000 impressions per hour. If the paint usually lasts three years, the salesman may be tempted to imply that it could last four or five years.

However, books written by professional salesmen caution that if a salesman makes a statement that the prospective buyer even suspects is overstated, he jeopardizes the sale, along with any future relationship with the customer.

The reason is simple. By exaggerating even once the salesman has signaled to the prospective buyer that he is sloppy with words. Thereafter, every statement the salesman makes will evoke a question in the buyer's mind: "Is this statement also an exaggeration?" Once the salesman informs us that words don't count, we, the buying public, have the right to discount all his claims.

Although in our daily family and social conversations we are not salespeople, we do want to be taken seriously. That will depend, in large part, on how we use words.

Let me tell you a story that illustrates this point. An 8-year-old boy has a neighbor over for the afternoon. Soon it's time for supper. The neighbor's mother calls, "Chaim, come home for supper!" Chaim continues to play. His mother calls him a second and third time. Chaim continues to play as if he didn't hear a thing. Finally, someone asks Chaim, "If your mother is calling you, why don't you go home?" Chaim answers in all sincerity, "Until my mother calls me seven times, she doesn't even mean it!" In effect, the mother has *taught* Chaim to discount her first six calls.

We all want to be respected. We want our advice to be sought, and our words to carry weight. But if we use sweeping words, if we respond with strong statements to minor situations, we teach people to discount our words.

The next time you have the opportunity to listen to an important person speak, listen to his or her choice of words. It's a powerful lesson in the accurate usage of words.

37.
RESPECT
Part One

Children are commanded to respect parents; students are commanded to respect *rebbes*; and we are all commanded to respect *rabbonim*. (It is, however, the responsibility of every parent, teacher, and rav, to facilitate and to make conducive this respect. This thought deserves a chapter to itself.)

This chapter is not addressing these relationships, but rather it focuses on the "respect" we have for each other, for our friends and neighbors. I am using the word "respect" to describe the esteem and regard in which a person is held.

There is a profound statement on the subject of respect that is important to know and internalize. Like many profound statements, it is true most of the time and we have to be careful not to allow the few exceptions to eclipse the truth. (When we evaluate material on personal growth, especially when it challenges something we have always believed, we tend to reject new material on the basis that it doesn't *always* apply! We are willing to overlook the 98 percent of the true application because of the 2 percent which is the exception. For the moment, until we have a chance to seriously consider the statement, please set aside the exception.)

It is very important to know and internalize that *for the most part, we teach people how to respect us!*

By the way we speak, walk, dress, act, and conduct ourselves with others, we say to the world: "I am someone important … Please treat me accordingly." Or we say, "I really don't think much of myself … You don't have to respect me any more than I respect myself."

The premise upon which this concept is built is that everything we do "teaches" others. Our actions send messages to everyone around us, and these messages really reflect what we think of ourselves and how we want to be treated by others.

To make this point, I offer a simple example: Reuven Chaim and Shimee are two young family men in their early 30's. They have been good friends since they can remember. In fact, they were born just two months apart.

Reuven Chaim was nicknamed "Ruby" by his siblings and friends. He thought this was cute until his 15th birthday, when he decided he wanted to be called by his full name, Reuven Chaim. He told his family and friends of his decision, and from that day on he didn't acknowledge anyone who called him by his nickname. There were some awkward moments, but in a short time his friends learned he really meant it and called him Reuven Chaim.

Shimee also wanted to be called by his full name, Elozer Shimon. In fact, it was his grandfather's name, and Shimee wanted to honor him. However, he continued to answer to Shimee. The message that his friends heard was, "Although I'd prefer to be called by my full name, it's okay if you call me Shimee." Since people would rather not change, everyone continued to call him Shimee.

It is only fair to say that Reuven Chaim and Shimee both *taught* everyone how to address them.

38.

RESPECT
Part Two

*I*n the previous chapter we introduced the concept that, for the most part, we *teach* people how to respect us. We project messages by the way we speak, walk, dress, act, and conduct ourselves with others. We told the story of two young men who had nicknames, and how only one of them was successful in teaching people that he wanted to be called by his full name.

Here are other examples of instructive behavior, with their meanings in parentheses:

- Speaking in a focused manner without babbling. (I take the time to think through what I want to say. I have it clear in my mind. Please address me accordingly.)

- Not reading, listening to, or watching mindless material. (I value my mind, and don't want it full of rubbish. Please don't offer me junk.)

- Referring to others by their appropriate title; referring to friends as "important people," not "the guys." (I value my friends. Please respect this, and treat me accordingly.)

- Coming on time for appointments. (I value my time and yours. Please respond accordingly.)

- Speaking with a positive, upbeat attitude. (I feel and work better with a positive attitude. Please don't dump negative things on me.)

- Not responding to a person blowing a car horn to get one's attention. (It can't be for me, because that's not how people address me.)

- Associating only with fine people. (I am an upright person, and feel comfortable only with people who have good values. Please don't make me uncomfortable by introducing me to unsavory people.)

- Making sure one's clothing is neat and clean. (People view me as a *talmid chacham,* so I have to dress the part. I want to be a walking *kiddush Hashem.* Please don't put me into a situation where I have to compromise my values.)

The Gemara tells us that (according to one version) a person who eats in the marketplace is not accepted by Jewish courts as a credible witness. Reb Aharon Kotler *zt"l* explains that a person who has little self-respect and behaves in an antisocial manner is untrustworthy and can even lie to the court. By eating in the marketplace, he announces to the world, "I don't respect myself," and we respond accordingly: "If you don't respect yourself, we can't respect you either."

Most of us want to blame others for any perceived lack of respect. "They don't respect me," we say. "They" could be a spouse, siblings, family, friends, congregants, students, co-workers, or anyone else with whom we deal. It is always easier to blame "them."

This new understanding really puts the blame for how "they" treat us directly on how we *taught* them to treat us.

Give this idea some thought … it may revolutionize your thinking.

39.
MESSAGES

"Your actions speak so loudly, I can't hear what you say!"

I want to dedicate this chapter to this simple yet profound concept, which is really the underpinning of our discussions of the last few chapters on interpersonal communication.

When we communicate with anyone, we do so on two separate levels. The first level is with the words we use, the verbal communication.

The second level is more complicated. It is made up of our facial expressions, tone of voice, body language, dress, even our stance. (It would be fair to say that science has yet to discover all the cues that a speaker projects. There may very well be subliminal cues that we can't yet detect or measure.)

We might think that our words are the predominant part of the message, and that the nonverbal cues just help to get the message across. In fact, just the opposite is true. The nonverbal cues create the majority of the impression! Studies have shown that as much as 70 to 80 percent of a listener's impression is created by the nonverbal messages. In simple English, this means that how you say something can be more important than what you say.

This is an astounding fact, and it should cause us to reflect on all the nonverbal messages we send when we speak.

But here is an even more interesting fact. When the listener is faced with two conflicting messages, when the verbal and nonverbal language are in contradiction, in almost all cases the nonverbal message is believed.

Professionals who study these subjects have always suspected the power of nonverbal communication, which was demonstrated clearly in the Nixon-Kennedy debate in 1959. This debate was heard on the radio by millions of people, and seen on television by millions. Extensive research was done on both groups, and the results were indisputable: 75 percent of the people who heard the debate on the radio said that Richard Nixon was the clear winner; and 75 percent who saw the debate on TV said that John Kennedy was the clear winner!

The reason for the discrepancy is simple. Nixon's logic and reasoning were superior, and so people who only heard the debate were convinced he won. But Kennedy's presentation — the confident look, the relaxed stance, the tailored suit, the tanned face, the smile — in essence, all the nonverbal messages — convinced people who watched the debate that his logic was better!

The message for us is loud and clear. The Almighty has created all of us with a sensitive "detector" which takes its cues not only from spoken words but from every other message that a speaker projects. When we hear something, we expect the way it was said to be in concert with what was said. When both are in "sync" our message is confirmed. When the way it is said is incompatible with the words, we struggle with it, and usually the nonverbal communication wins.

How true it is that "your actions speak so loudly, I can't hear what you say."

40.

SUCCESS

Part One

Could there be a "formula" for success, or would that violate some basic principle or *hashkafah* (religious value system)?

Let's talk about building a house. Say that I own a nice, level piece of land and decide to build a house for my family on it. I approach a friend who does general contracting and ask him to build the house for me.

He would ask me, "What type and size house do you want, and do you have architectural plans?"

Assume that I would answer him, "No, I don't have any plans ... and I don't need any! We'll just design and build the house as we go along! We'll wing it!"

My contractor friend may think I'm off the wall to build a house without plans ... but to humor me, he agrees.

On the first day we stake out an area 50 x 30 feet and bring in a bulldozer to excavate a basement. After pouring a cement wall, I decide to have an indoor garage, so we break the wall and create a driveway from the basement to the street.

We start to build the first floor. After the walls go up, I realize that the dining room is too small, so I decide to add another few feet to the house to extend it. Again we have to excavate a new foundation, take down existing walls, and build a new wall.

You can easily see that this house will become a comedy of errors. Each change means destroying something already built. The cost of this house would be phenomenal, many times the cost of building from a plan. The end product would not be structurally sound, because it would consist of patchwork; and when it came to selling the house, few people would want it without a central theme. It would be a random collection of rooms ... not a home.

So far I haven't told you anything that you don't already know. You need plans to build a house!

But here is an interesting point. In a recently built home, the builder, working from a good set of plans, made over a *dozen* changes. We might ask him why he needed plans if he had to make over a dozen changes to them. Why couldn't he just build?

The contractor's answer would be readily forthcoming. "The changes made in the plans are relatively small changes. If I had no plans, I'd be shooting in the dark. I'd have no direction."

The lesson here is simple. The fact that we deviate from plans is no reason not to make them. The oft-heard excuse, "What good are plans anyway when I have to make changes?" is not a well thought-out concept.

Just as a contractor is always better off following a plan, notwithstanding the changes he may have to make, so are we better off in any given project with a clearly thought-out plan — notwithstanding the changes that we will have to make.

41.
SUCCESS
Part Two

*I*n the last chapter we presented the importance of having an architect's plan before beginning to build a house, in spite of the fact that we know there will be many changes along the way.

Have you ever been personally involved in building a house?

Here is what happens on a daily basis. The general contractor comes early and reviews the work that was finished the previous day. He inspects the quality and amount of work completed by each tradesman. He then refers to the plans in order to lay out the day's work. For example, if the concrete for the foundation was poured two days ago and is now hard, then today's work might be to construct the first floor.

The contractor meets with the carpenters, reviews the plans with them, and decides where and how to start. He checks to make sure that the necessary materials have been delivered to the site.

If yesterday's work was to complete the "framing-up" of the house and today's work is putting up sheetrock, the contractor consults with the plans and determines exactly where the sheetrock is to be put, where the spaces for the doors and windows are to be left, and where the appliances will be installed.

The contractor and the tradesmen consult the building plans every morning before begining their work, and many times during the day. In fact, you can walk onto any building site and you will see the plans spread out, readily available to each person involved.

When the house is finally complete, do we congratulate the contractor on his "good luck"? Do we view this completed house as a "miracle"? Not really! We take for granted that when plans are carefully made, and patiently, consistently, and proficiently followed, with Hashem's help the project will be completed.

Because building a house is an unusually good example of how carefully drawn plans translate into a finished product, we have explained it in detail. Also, the building of a house allows the workers to see the fruits of their daily labors materialize before their eyes. Two carpenters who start at 7 a.m. can frame several rooms by late afternoon. They can actually see how the 2x4 pieces of lumber which were in a pile yesterday are now the studs of a wall. The viewer can see how an area was divided, with walls, windows and doors put into place. This morning they stood on an open floor; by late afternoon they stand in a house.

That's progress and it provides a great feeling of accomplishment. This may be one reason why construction of new homes is so exciting!

Although in other fields — education, music, sports, etc. — we can't see the progress as dramatically as we can in the building of a house, the progress from plans to a finished product is no less effective.

The lesson gleaned from the building industry is one that we could, and should, apply to every area: We accomplish more, better, and faster when we follow a plan.

42.
SUCCESS
Part Three

*I*n the last two chapters we discussed the need for a formula and a plan in order to achieve success. Today I would like to discuss the formula.

The formula is surprisingly easy to outline, but a little more difficult to follow. It consists of five steps.

1. Decide exactly what you want. Those few words may sound so simple, yet many people can't decide what they want because in doing so they are excluding so many other choices. Choosing A, B, C, D, or E locks them into a choice. Now that they have chosen, they have to perform. As long as they vacillate among all the choices, they don't have to come through.

Deciding exactly what you want is synonymous with the architect saying, "Decide on the size of the room. Will it be 12x16 or 16x20? Because only after you decide on the size can I draw plans, and only then can the contractor order supplies."

The plan has to be written to be of value. Our minds are capable of thinking so many thoughts in so short a time that they are fleeting memories only 10 seconds later. Writing crystallizes thoughts. In writing a plan, we are sending our own mind the message that this is "for real."

There are many stories of people who took the time and effort to write down what they wanted and were surprised at how many things on their list actually came to pass.

Some years ago, Torah Umesorah asked me to teach *kollel* men during the summer *bein hazmanim*. Between sessions I sat in the shade and read a book. A good friend, who was the principal of a fledgling school, came by and, in a whimsical tone called out to me, "Avi, tell me what good book you are reading so I can get smart too!" I answered him in the same whimsical tone, "When you show me your list of eleven personal growth plans, I'll be happy to add the book I'm reading as the twelfth."

That must have gotten his attention because he walked across the field toward me and said, "Avi, what are you talking about?"

I patiently explained to him the value and power of writing down a list of things he could do to become a better principal, and I challenged him to compose one for himself.

There was just one condition. His list of self-improvement ideas had to be composed without the usual limitations of time and money. The real question became: If you had the time and resources that you needed for this project, what would you do?

He sat down, and for the next half hour was lost in deep thought. He didn't write, he didn't talk to me, he just sat and thought. Most likely this was the first time he had been challenged by such a question.

Slowly, thoughtfully, he began to write a list. Finally, he handed me a list of eleven ideas, including classes to visit in various schools, books and articles to read, cassettes to listen to, and people to meet. It was a well thought-out list with names of people, authors, lecturers, and educators.

In turn, I gave him the name of the book I was reading, we exchanged pleasantries, and he left.

Eight months later I met him at the Torah Umesorah convention, where he proudly told me that already he had fulfilled ten of the twelve items on his list. Here at the convention, he had made an appointment with a certain rav who was one of the two remaining people to see on his list.

A written list is a wonderful way to concretize what you really want.

43.
SUCCESS
Part Four

*I*n our last chapter I discussed the first item in the five-part formula for success: "Decide exactly what you want."

2. Step two is to clearly and completely picture what you want, and to write it down. How clearly and completely should this be written?

The answer to this question is best understood by carefully looking at an architect's plans. When you read these plans you will see that they have been drawn so comprehensively that any craftsman can follow them, almost without further instructions! In other words, the thinking and planning have already been done and are represented in the plans; now all that is left is for the craftsmen to follow the plans faithfully.

In no way do I mean to deprecate the work of the craftsmen. The carpenter's expertise will make all the difference in whether a door is framed properly or not, whether a window is hung correctly or at a slight angle. The skill of each craftsman will ultimately determine the quality of the finished house. The point I want to make is that the overall design of the house, the size and function of each room, the building materials, the layout, and the "flow" of the house are the domain of the architect.

We can go one step further. In the mind's eye of the architect, once the plans of the house have been meticulously drawn, once he visualizes the house, it is built. The fact that the foundation has yet to be excavated, the frame has yet to be put up, and the roof has yet to be built are minor details to a person who visualizes the house mentally.

That is the special fringe benefit you get from a crystal-clear, written goal. The vision of the finished house becomes a powerful motivation! The vision of the completed house becomes the incentive for the builder and the owner, and helps them overcome problems and obstacles. When there is no clear picture, they lose this necessary drive.

Another way to describe this concept would be to watch a master painter at work. After considerable thought he will outline the picture that he has in his mind. He may position the major elements of the drawing with just a few strokes. For example, if he is painting a farm scene, he may choose to outline the road, main house, barn, and fields.

After that has been done, what remains is the painstaking work of filling in the lines. The ultimate quality of the painting will, of course, be determined by how masterfully this work is done — the choice of colors, the sharpness of detail, the cleanliness of lines — but the basic picture was already determined in the artist's mind with the initial strokes.

Many years ago I read a story about a man who wandered into the kitchen of a restaurant and found two people washing dishes. He asked the first person what he was doing and got the obvious answer: "I'm washing dishes." He then asked the same question to the second person and was told, "I am working my way through medical school by washing dishes."

I think it is fair to say that the first person was just doing something to earn a few dollars, indifferently throwing some paint on his canvas. The second person was also working to make a few dollars, but at the same time he was carefully and thoughtfully filling paint into the lines on his canvas. Perhaps both people were doing the same manual work, but because of a master plan — or lack of it — the work had totally different meaning to each of them.

44.
SUCCESS
Part Five

In creating a formula for success, I have discussed two steps:

1. Decide on what you want.

2. Clearly picture it, and write it down.

We're now ready for step three:

3. Discover how others have done it.

I once took a course in which the instructor held up a piece of paper and told us, "I will guarantee that everyone who meticulously follows what's written on this paper will succeed in any endeavor they undertake!"

That got my attention!

Surprisingly, the piece of paper had just a few questions.

a) Describe exactly what you want.

b) Assuming that what you want to do has already been done by others, ask five people who have done it to tell you what they did. What did these people read? To whom did they listen? What classes did they attend? What skills did they acquire?

After you have the answers from five people, correlate them to see which ones are most logical and relevant for you at this time.

What we have now are a set of "tracks," a very important aid to help you head in the right direction.

When I taught first grade, I was fascinated by the children's endless questions. At that age, their minds were open to the excitement of the world around them, and their creativity was at a peak. One day, out of the clear blue sky, one of the boys asked me, "Rebbe, why do trains needs tracks?" I asked him the reason for the question, and he told me that since the train was so big, so strong, and could go anywhere, why did it need tracks? Let it just go!

One important answer is as follows: It's only because someone has clearly designated the place for the train by laying tracks that the train can go where *we* want it to go. If there were no tracks, the train would go where *it* wanted to go, not where *we want it to go.*

Once you have tracks, you still need power. But whether the train goes fast or slow, or even if it stops for a while, as long as it follows its "tracks" it will eventually reach its destination.

The information you will gather from the five successful people you interview — the books they read, the things they did — becomes your set of tracks.

I once taught this concept to a group of students, and then to give the lesson a dramatic flavor, I brought a battery-operated train into class. First I ran the train on a tabletop with no tracks. The engine immediately veered off to the side and I caught it just as it was about to go off the table.

I then placed tracks on the table and again ran the engine. This time, of course, it ran across the table, just where it was supposed to go.

When an obstacle, such as a pencil or small book, was placed in front of the train without tracks, the engine was deflected. When the tracks went over the obstacles, the engine easily continued in its true course.

A simple, almost childlike demonstration of the value of "tracks" is a powerful way to get the message clearly understood.

45.
SUCCESS
Part Six

This chapter is the last in the "Success" series. We have attempted to develop a simple formula for succeeding in a given project, course of study, skill-building, or, for that matter, in any area. What we have covered so far is the need to decide on what you want, clearly picture it and write it down, and discover how others have done it. We suggested that a person lay "tracks" to point him in the right direction. We're now ready for the fourth step.

4. Make a commitment in time, effort, and money. More easily said than done, because first we have to make room for this commitment.

To be effective, to really get this to work, we have to make sure that there won't be a conflicting project or program that will make it difficult for us to make our new commitment. For example, if we want to start a new course of study twice a week, we first have to ask ourselves, "What have I been doing until now in that time?" We have to be willing to make the trade-off, to invest the time, effort, and, when applicable, the money.

To believe that we can gain desirable results *without* any investments of time, energy, or money (or all three) is unrealistic, and an invitation to frustration.

There are no "free lunches" or, for that matter, any other free meal. Therefore, achievement of our objective requires trade-offs. Let's list them.

The *time* we spend working on this project will limit how much time we can spend on other projects, so list the time involved.

Monies invested in this project must be taken from income, savings, or investments; list the financial sources.

The *energy* we will expend to complete this project must curtail the energy available for our other activities; list the current activities.

This process of listing the trade-offs will force you to think through carefully, step by step, how you will see your project to fruition. You may find, to your surprise, that the price of time, energy, or money is prohibitive at this time, and you may therefore choose to postpone this project to a later date. If this was done objectively, you saved yourself a lot of heartache. But if you do decide to go ahead, you will be prepared and raise the probability of succeeding.

Now we come to the last of our steps:

5. Review and upgrade your commitment weekly.

Making the commitment is the easy part. Following through is where most of us fall down.

The advice of people who have made the dynamics of success their life study is to set aside a few minutes every week to review your progress. Ten minutes in quiet thought every week — perhaps on Motza'ei Shabbos — will reawaken the excitement that you had when you first thought of the project, and will help you over the hurdles.

You may find it of value to list all of the benefits you can possibly imagine in completing this project successfully, and to review this list when you check your progress. The trick here is to list not only the obvious benefits, but to really "reach" even for the obscure advantages. When you face the difficult moments, when your enthusiasm is at a low, you will need as many benefits as you can think of to get you going again. At that time, your long list becomes a valuable motivation.

So we have come full circle. We started this discussion by first deciding exactly what we want. We went on to picture it clearly, in full detail. We asked others who have successfully completed such a project how they did it, and we used their advice as the "tracks" for our own path. Now that we know what the steps are, we have to think carefully and decide if we are ready to pay the price in time, energy, and money, and what the trade-offs will be.

The final step is to devise some system whereby we can monitor our progress weekly and re-energize our committment.

Is there a formula for success that will work every time? No. However, if carefully followed, these five points will considerably increase the chance of success, and that's a lot!

46.
A GREAT FIGHT

I recently witnessed a great disagreement that escalated into a good argument and then into a "great fight." All of this, mind you, was motivated, if you believed the principals of both sides, entirely *l'shem Shamayim* (for the sake of the Almighty's honor).

Each person had strong convictions, believing that not only was he right but that his only reason for getting into the fight was to protect and advance the Almighty's honor.

After carefully listening to both sides of the argument, I had an interesting question. How does one really know if an argument is *l'shem Shamayim* or not?

After asking a number of people, I would like to offer two ways to test if a "fight" is indeed *l'shem Shamayim.*

Many of us remember the story of Chanah, who was childless, and her co-wife Peninah (both were married to Elchonon), who had ten children.

Every time the family went up to Yerushalayim for a Yom Tov, Peninah would goad Chanah by asking her if she had brought clothing and presents for her (nonexistent) children. Peninah's intent was to provoke Chanah to pray to the Almighty so intently, so meaningfully, for children that she would be answered. And that is exactly what happened. Peninah's goading touched Chanah so deeply, caused a hurt in her soul so painful, that her prayers were answered, and a son, later to become Shmuel the Prophet, was born to her.

It would seem that this problem was resolved so beautifully — or was it? Our *Chachamim* tells us that because Peninah hurt Chanah deeply, she was punished! In spite of the fact that Peninah meant well, in spite of the fact that her ultimate objective was reached, she was harshly punished!

The lesson here is quite simple and powerful. When you pain someone, regardless of how noble your intentions and how successful you are, you are no longer doing the will of the Almighty.

So your first question to yourself should be, "Is anyone going to be hurt in this disagreement?" If the answer is yes, regardless of your lofty motivation and your "holy" intent, consider that this might not be the fulfillment of the Almighty's desire.

The second criterion is an interesting observation made by the Gemara *Yevamos*. Hillel and Shammai are the optimal example of two people whose argument was *l'shem Shamayim*. In fact, they are the example heralded by the Mishnah in *Pirkei Avos*, where this idea is developed. The Gemara teaches us that although the students of Hillel and Shammai had great disagreements on some of the fundamental laws of marriage, these disagreements did not prevent them from joining together on every level.

If an argument is so divisive that it prevents the participants from remaining friends, it may have overstepped the boundaries of *l'shem Shamayim*.

47.
A BEAUTIFUL LETTER

*I*t may take years before the impact of a program that serves people is known and fully appreciated.

A case in point is the S.E.E.D. program that I was privileged to direct for Torah Umesorah for over twenty years. The idea was quite simple: *Kollel* couples and *beis medrash bochurim* would go to a community for several weeks during *bein hazmanim* and learn with local people. The impact on the *ba'lei batim* with whom they learned, on the youngsters in the community whom they befriended, and on the families whom they impressed takes years to unfold. Surprisingly, it is the *kollel* couples themselves — the very people who went to teach — who often tell me how much they learned. In Hebrew we have the expression, "He came to teach and found himself a student."

I am presenting a letter from just such a couple who now belong to an evergrowing number of community *kollelim*. I have purposely omitted the names of the various communities to protect the identity of the writer.

Dear Mr. Shulman:

You may remember us from a S.E.E.D. program of six years ago when we went to the West Coast. These few weeks gave us a taste for "going out to do the work for Klal Yisrael."

Since then we have been in kollel in the Midwest and are enjoying the opportunity to be in the forefront of building a community.

One of the obstacles that we have encountered in both our S.E.E.D. work and here in the outreach work of the kollel is that ideas are met with the attitude: "It won't work … don't even bother to try … because of XYZ."

We have been trying to first think big and then see if all the details can be put into place. We have noticed that most people operate in the opposite order — not allowing themselves to seriously consider a project because of a detail. Our method works — it has met with much success, and also with many scoffers.

It was therefore a big chizuk for us to read your column in the Yated Ne'eman about thinking big and the "malach" which you created. That column and the follow-up one were especially heartwarming because they validated our method of overcoming problems.

Somehow, I would call it hashgachah, many impossible details have fallen into place. That imaginary "malach" that you say you invented to take care of problems really does exist … but if you don't start your project, then you will never encounter the malach.

We greatly enjoy your articles and books.

Very truly yours,
Kollel Couple

You're right on target. Thank you.

48.
ANIYIM TABLE

A friend sent along a letter that he had received three weeks before his son's bar mitzvah. Together with the letter was an elegant, beautifully embossed "tent card" for each guest table at the affair. The tent card, in just a few sentences, described the work of "Tomchei Shabbos" and the concept of an aniyim table — a special table set aside to feed poor people.

Dear Mr. and Mrs. Goldberg:

Mazel Tov on Eli's forthcoming bar mitzvah.
Recently my husband and I were invited to watch Tomchei Shabbos volunteers prepare food packages for needy families. It was an exhilarating experience.

As we watched, we were reminded of an old, beautiful custom of inviting poor people to actually eat at the simchah — it was called an aniyim table. In many communities, at every simchah there was a special table set aside where poor people came to eat. While our lifestyle doesn't allow for poor people to actually come and join the simchah, the idea occurred to us — why not revive the custom by purchasing food packages for delivery to needy people the Shabbos of the simchah?

Can you imagine the wonderful feeling you would have knowing that the very Shabbos of your son's simchah you also provided food for needy families? It is as if you would have invited these families as guests to your simchah.

The logistics are simple — purchase any number of packages at $33 each (that will feed a family of two adults and 4 children for Shabbos, plus) and designate the Thursday your packages should be delivered — Tomche Shabbos volunteers will do all the rest.

Again, wishing you a heartfelt mazel tov, I remain,

Very truly yours,

A volunteer

P.S. Please find a return envelope for your convenience. Also please note the "tent cards" that are available to be placed at each seudah table.

My friend made a donation equivalent to inviting six couples to his *seudah*.

He was so inspired by the mitzvah of *tzedakah* and the opportunity to revive an old *minhag* that he spoke about it in his speech to the bar mitzvah boy.

Subsequently, he heard stories of people who donated the equivalent cost of a wedding to help an orphan get married in Israel and of a family who made a bar mitzvah and purchased *tefillin* for other boys at the same time.

A minhag of *Klal Yisrael* is precious; what a *zchus* it is to revive it.

In keeping with an age-old custom of inviting the needy to eat at simchas, your hosts have graciously purchased Tomchei Shabbos seudos to be delivered

on _____.

49.
PEER PRESSURE
Part One

arents whose daughter attends an out-of-town girls high school asked me to help them deal with their children's peer pressure. They wanted to know how and when to say, "I don't care what your friends do. I want you to do this," and survive! How could they convey to their daughter that they knew what was best in spite of what all her friends were doing?

What led to this speech was one mother's paralyzing fear that her 16-year-old daughter didn't yet possess the maturity to drive a car. The young girl had taken driving lessons and knew the fundamentals, but in the mother's opinion didn't have the discretion needed for safe driving. The mother had no doubt that this discretion would come with normal development in the next few years, but at this moment the girl didn't have it. In addition, since there was bus service to and from school in this community, and several of this girl's older friends offered to take her shopping and to programs, the mother could not justify putting a dangerous 3,000-pound machine into the hands of her daughter. Why should she risk her daughter's, and others', safety?

When she consulted mothers of her daughter's classmates, she was amazed to find that many of them expressed the very same apprehension — but shrugged off their fears with the remark, "But everyone does it, so what can we do?"

The mother went to the principal of the school to ask him to consider making it school policy that no girl drive before she is 18 years old. The principal told her that this was not a school issue, but rather a parenting issue which required parents to take a position and to use the terrible word "NO!" Moreover, he told her that it was only because parents didn't have the intestinal fortitude (in simple English, guts) to say no, that they wanted the school to be the "bad guy." He refused, but in a conciliatory move offered to invite me to address the school's parent body.

The term "peer pressure" applies not only to school children but to all of us. Children, teenagers, and adults are all affected by the pressure exerted by friends, neighbors, colleagues, co-workers, and business associates — our peers. The Rambam states that a person is "drawn after his friend," which means that he has a basic desire to do as everyone else does, not to be different, not to stand out.

Peer pressure can be advantageous, because when a person surrounds himself with a group of fine, upright, respectable people, the pressure to do as they do will elevate him. But the opposite is also true. Join a group of dishonest, disrespectful people, and they will exert a negative influence.

But we all have a measure of individualism as well. We don't want to become exactly like other people. And here is the balancing act: On one hand, we want to blend in, to be alike; and on the other hand, we want to retain our individualism. This tug of war goes on all the time at almost every age, but it is especially powerful during the teen years.

We will discuss some further thoughts on peer pressure in the next chapter. As an introduction I would like to tell you a story.

Years ago my father *zt"l* took me to our small local bank, where my father met with the president and obtained a signature-loan of several thousand dollars. When I expressed amazement that a bank would loan money or issue credit just on a signature, with no security, my father explained that he had a relationship with this bank president that spanned over two decades. My father had borrowed various amounts of money many times, and had repaid each loan to the day, sometimes even earlier than he had to! In the process, my father slowly built a relationship of trust. The lesson I learned was that it takes years to develop credit. You can't walk into a bank and say, "Okay, I'm here; give me my credit!"

To a large extent, the same applies in other relationships, including those between parents and children. Trust, like credit, takes years to develop, especially to the point where one can expect to be trusted simply on his word.

50.
PEER PRESSURE
Part Two

*I*n the last chapter I introduced a basic foundation in dealing with the peer pressure our children experience — namely, building trust. We pointed out that building trust between two people is similar to building credit in a bank. In both cases you can't have it instantly; rather, it has to be built up over years.

A child's trust in a parent develops from hundreds and thousands of experiences where the parent has kept his word, been fair, kept a confidence, believed in the child's ability, admitted he didn't know something when he was wrong. It also means that the parent was forthright and open in his criticism, never sarcastic.

The sum total of such a relationship is trust. The child knows that his parents have only his welfare at heart, are sensitive in their decisions, and most of the time are right.

Every family has its own value system. How we greet each other, how we *daven*, what we discuss at our supper table, whether we invite guests to join us for our Shabbos meals, and thousands of other actions add up to a family value system.

In addition to what we do, a family value system is expressed by what parents believe. For example, parents may believe that cheating is wrong. If this issue was discussed at various, non-confrontational times over a period of years, with numerous examples of how wrong it is to cheat, and what happens to people who succumb to the temptation to cheat, if the halachic and ethical points have been discussed ... we now have a firmly established family value. (It goes without saying that we assume the parents practice their values in their daily lives.)

For the most part — and we realize there will be exceptions — a child who has bought into his parents' way of life, who sees the high repute and respect his parents enjoy, will have an automatic mental reflex to the word "cheating." He will think: "Our family doesn't do that."

I remember a few years ago a friend told me the following story. He was in a park when a teenage Bais Yaakov girl asked him to loan her a dime to call her mother (now you know how old this story is), promising to return the dime as soon as her mother came to pick her up. When he gave her the dime, he said, "Just keep it; you don't have to return it." She looked at him and said, "That's not the way our family does it. I'll return the money to you," and she did.

What is important is that the child should know specifically what his parents' value system is. Unfortunately, many times I have asked young children and teenagers what their parents' position would be on a particular issue, and was told either that their parents had expressed no position, or that they had no clear position (sometimes yes, sometimes no), or that they had an entirely unrealistic position. In these situations the parents have not gotten across to the child, and as a result the child has not bought into the parents' values.

In most situations, strong, logical family values that are clearly defined, openly discussed, reinforced often, and practiced by the family will result in a value system that children will accept.

I think it is reasonable to say that one of the most powerful allies a parent can have in helping a child overcome peer pressure is the trust that the child has in the parent's decisions.

51.
PEER PRESSURE
Part Three

*I*n the last two chapters we discussed building trust and developing family values. Today we will try to explain how the family value system can help defuse tense situations that may arise as a result of a teenage child's pressure to conform to peer standards.

Most of us don't want to be taken by surprise. If there are to be new rules, if my office is going to be changed, if I am going to have to do something differently, I want to know about it in advance. One of the reasons is that I want to have time to adjust to the change (whether or not I like it).

Imagine a scenario where all of your daughter's 16-year-old friends are getting their driving permits, and she is anxiously awaiting her birthday so that she too can get her permit. All of a sudden, you decide to tell her, "Sorry, you can't get your permit and license until you're 18!" You can probably imagine the reaction: "Why am I different? If all my friends can, why can't I?"

You can let your imagination add the appropriate dramatics: yelling, screaming, crying, or just sulking to fit a particular situation as needed.

I can't promise you that you'll win the discussion each time, and that your son or daughter will readily accept your decision in spite of what their friends do, but when the family values of responsibility and safety have been discussed over the years, well before the issue of getting a license arises, your chances of prevailing will increase dramatically.

The most difficult situation is when you're in a confrontation mode. Then it becomes "my needs versus your position," and you and your child can hardly hear each other. Contrast that with a theoretical discussion which is unrelated to the actual event. You're simply discussing a concept; it's not you against your child, it's an idea that you're talking about. At this point both parties can "hear" and understand each other more readily.

Following are some expressions that commonly arise when topics of conflict are discussed by parents and their children.

■ All My Friends …

We tend to speak in sweeping generalities. "They all said" means two people said. "In response to the overwhelming requests" means two people asked for it (one of them the speaker's mother)!

"All my friends" may mean a small group, but not necessarily "all." Moreover, we need to know which group, and why. In a number of situations, parents have been successful in thwarting the onslaught of "all my friends" by speaking to some parents and finding that they too are taking a strong position against something they really don't want for their child. By speaking with a few parents, you may find that common sense prevails.

■ Our Family

The statement "Our family does it this way" has significant meaning if the family does many things: some exciting, some interesting, some fun, and also some that are restrictive. A child can buy into the package. We can reason with him that he enjoys going on family trips and participating in family activities, and the flip side of that is that he has to abide by the family restrictions as well.

But if the family does not do any exciting, interesting, or fun things, and the only time the concept "our family" is used is in a negative sense (i.e.,"we don't"), your chances of convincing the child of the importance of a restriction are much less. In his mind, you are using the "family" as a copout to get what you want.

When a child sees fairness and balance, he is much more likely to respect family practices and proudly adhere to them.

Recently a young lady of 20 came to our house and in conversation happened to mention that her parents would not allow her to drive until she was 19 years old. When I asked her if it was difficult for her not to drive when all her friends drove, she answered, "Yes, it was hard, but I was happy to please my parents. They're so special!"

That's a gratifying payback for years of building trust.

52.
MY BROTHER
Part One

I was sitting at the table at a wedding when a man came over and introduced himself to me. After a few minutes of casual conversation it occurred to me that he wanted to speak to me about something serious and his small talk was just meant to warm him up to the subject.

Finally he said, "Could I please share a very personal story with you?" Before I had a chance to answer, he was off and running.

"As I am getting older — I am nearly 70 — I am rethinking my many associations. I am remembering friends that I had decades ago and considering what happened to us over the years. Many of them just drifted away, they moved and we only saw each other several times; slowly some went away from Torah and mitzvos and I decided to allow our previous close friendship to wane.

"As you grow older your circle of friends continually changes and I imagine that this is the way of the world. But there is one person whom I genuinely liked but with whom I couldn't continue a friendship."

My table partner took a long breath and I knew I was in for a story.

"This particular person is a cousin about my age, and it is because of my brother that I decided to break my friendship with my cousin. When I was much younger, my brother, who was two years older than I, had many questions about *Yiddishkeit*. Although our parents' home was *shomer shabbos,* it wasn't enough to hold him.

"He eventually left the house and married a totally nonreligious woman. My parents were understandably heartbroken. They cried for days and didn't go out of the house for weeks. Slowly they resumed their life.

"My cousin was fascinated by my brother's activities, and my parents' reaction. Every time we would meet, after asking me a few perfunctory questions, he would revert back to questions about my brother. Had we heard from him? Was he still married? Did he have children? etc…

"Although I told him numerous times that the subject pained me, and to please not ask me about him, he somehow always found his way back to a discussion about my brother. It came to the point that I choose not to invite him to our house, even to family *simchahs*.

"This cousin never did well in life. His religious beliefs were superficial, his family life was dysfunctional, and he always struggled to make a living. Years later it occurred to me that perhaps his constant questions to me were not so much out of great interest, but rather to bring up a subject that would put me down and thus 'bring him up.' As long as he could flaunt the fact that I had a non-religious brother, then in his mind I couldn't feel superior to him. To the contrary, notwithstanding his own personal inadequacies, because all of his siblings were full-fledged members of *Klal Yisrael*, he was so much better than I.

"Now that I have this understanding, which I am pretty certain is right, I have more compassion rather than animosity toward him. I realize that all he wanted to do was hide his own shortcomings and use my brother as convenient cover."

When he finished this story, he took a long drink of water and just sat quietly.

53.
MY BROTHER
Part Two

*I*n the last chapter I told a story of a guest I had met at a wedding.

This man's brother wasn't religious and his cousin constantly brought up the subject. This became so painful that the man finally ended his friendship with his cousin. Now, years later, the man realized that his cousin's real intent was not so much to annoy him as to cover up his own inadequacies. By continually referring to the irreligious brother, the cousin was sending a message: "You too have dirty linen, so the fact that I have my failings is not so bad."

After patiently listening to his story, I asked my newly acquired friend if he had any questions to ask me, and he said, "No, I don't." He just wanted to find an understanding person with whom to share his story.

He may not have had any questions for me, but his story started me thinking anyway.

I began to wonder if I ever bring up an unpleasant subject when I'm talking to a friend, with the subconscious message, "Since I don't have the same problem as you do, I am obviously better than you!"

I was reminded of an incident that must have happened years ago. I had just started a teaching job and a group of us were driving to school. One *rebbe* said that for some reason he was unprepared to teach a certain subject that day and was going to "wing" it. Although this *rebbe* had been teaching for more years than I was old, I blurted out, "I would never teach anything without preparation."

After I had made that brilliant statement, I immediately knew that I had said something wrong. The cold looks that all the *rebbes* gave me verified that.

Later that day at recess, a *rebbe* who had been in the car that morning took me aside and explained to me that what I had said was a classic example of "honoring oneself through the shame of his friend."

The *aveirah* of honoring yourself at someone else's expense is interesting because it applies even when your only intent is to raise your own esteem in front of another and you do not intend to demean your friend's honor. For example, I might say that I have $10,000 in savings, which is more than the $5,000 that Shimon has. Although Shimon's sum is not shameful, nevertheless, I have used Shimon as a tool (perhaps the word "stepstool" would be more accurate) to enhance myself, and that is not allowed.

The competitiveness of our business, social, and educational systems are such that we are often tempted to rate or score ourselves against someone else. "My raise was larger than Joe's, our car is better than our neighbors', my son is doing better than Chaim" are all common examples where we use someone else to measure our own position.

In addition to the unhealthy psychological implications, using any person to bolster our esteem is halachically wrong.

Consider this the next time you are tempted to compare.

54.
MISHNAYOS
Part One

*I*t is an unusual opportunity to have a gadol hador live in your community, where you can listen to him teach, observe him, and occasionally consult with him.

We in Monsey had just such an opportunity when Rabbi Yaakov Kamenetzky zt"l moved within a block of our home, where the Rosh Yeshiva and the rebbitzen lived for seventeen years.

As a result of a discussion with the Rosh Yeshiva about the importance of learning Mishnayos, I convinced six boys to learn for a half hour on Shabbos and Sunday afternoon, and we started a Mishnayos group.

Over the next few years I was asked by many mechanchim and parents to tell them the value and procedure of teaching Mishnayos to children. As a result I wrote an article which was published in the November 1980 Jewish Observer, titled Mishnayos: A Course of Study for Young and Old.

Over the last two decades, Mishnayos has become more popular in some circles, and less popular with others. Some of the points made in the article are even more important today than when they were written. I want to share the article with you as it appeared in the Jewish Observer.

"Mishnayos: A Course of Study for Young and Old."

"Mishanayos? Not anymore!... I'm 11 years old, I learn Gemara!"

My interest in Mishnayos developed quite by accident. I was studying in a *beis medrash* where two 15-year-old *bochurim* learning *Maseches Kiddushin* were having a heated argument about a *din* of *shlichus* (an aspect of the principle of designating an agent). The argument was so long and loud that I could not help overhearing it, and I was amazed to discover that their dispute was a result of simple ignorance of a clearly stated fact in a Mishnah in *Gittin*.

It was disturbing: Why should 15-year-old boys — or anybody, for that matter — be frustrated in their independent study for not having learned a Mishnah? Then, more directly, what can be done to encourage the next generation of *talmidim* to overcome the same problem?

Subsequently, I discussed the general topic of learning Mishnayos with *roshei yeshiva*, *menahalim*, *rebbeim*, and parents, and the following observations emerged from their comments:

As is known, Moshe Rabbeinu received both the *Torah She'b'ksav* (Written Law) and the *Torah She'b'alpeh* (the Oral Law) at Sinai. The latter was transmitted from teacher to disciple from memory. Some thirteen centuries later, Rabbeinu HaKadosh (Rabbi Yehuda HaNasi/the prince) saw the need to transcribe Torah Sheb'alpeh. In the few sentences that comprise each Mishnah, Rabbeinu HaKadosh conveyed the essence of *halachah*; and this was further expanded upon and clarified in the discussions and debates of the Gemara recorded several centuries later. Thus, Mishnah is in every sense both the base and the framework of the Gemara.

The Mishnayos Advantages:
For Both Children and Adults

Because the Mishnah is written in relatively simple, classic Hebrew — especially when compared to the Gemara's Aramaic — its language and message can be more easily grasped by the inexperienced student. Moreover, the form of the Mishnah — the presentation of one or several related thoughts in each Mishnah — is conducive to easier comprehension than Gemara, even to a young child. Thus every novice can handle the basic thought presented in a Mishnah without the extra complications of language or extended debate associated with the Gemara. As the student grows and develops, the *peirush* of Rav (Rabbi Ovadiah of Bartenura's definitive commentary) should be added to his course of study so that he continues to grow in the depth of his undersanding as he advances in experience and maturity.

55.

MISHNAYOS
Part Two

*I*n the last chapter I related a conversation with Rav Yaakov Kamenetzky zt"l about the importance of learning Mishnayos. This chapter continues with some ideas.

Study of Mishnah has yet another advantage. A complete unit of thought is encapsuled in each Mishnah, allowing one to cover a meaningful amount of Mishnayos in the space of only a few minutes. This affords the younger student — even one of limited attention span — the opportunity to satisfy the deep, often unfulfilled, emotional need to pursue a project to completion, tasting from a variety of subjects over a relatively short span of time. This is also attractive to the ambitious adult or seasoned scholar with an overtaxed schedule. It is well known, for example, that Rabbi Moshe Feinstein, venerated as our leading authority in *halachah*, has long made it a practice to review several chapters of Mishnayos every day, as he put away his *tefillin*.

An "Open Door" Reward

More must be said about the value of the study of Mishnayos to a young student. The fact that it opens the door to sections of *Shas* (the full Talmud) that the average student following the conventional curriculum may not learn for another ten years, gives him an appreciable measure of satisfacion and self-esteem. Equally important is the practical "hard nosed" benefit to the *talmid* when "making a *laynen*" (approaching a new piece of Gemara independently before hearing a lecture on it); even a good student can become frustrated when dealing with the Gemara's quoting of a totally unfamiliar Mishnah. Not only is the content of the quote often vague and confusing, as is the Gemara's entire discusion, the novice is dealing with concepts and language that are often unclear. One can visualize the frustration and wasted effort this can cause — especially when the time-frame or the general trend of the Gemara's discussion does not allow for leisurely exploration of the quoted Mishnah. By contrast, the student who has learned a considerable amount of Mishnayos will not be thwarted by a quote of a concept from even an unfamiliar Gemara. While he may not have learned the specific quotation, his broad familiarity with topics discussed in *Shas*, culled from his knowledge of Mishnayos, has given him the "working tools" to understand the Gemara's reference.

It is for this reason that Rabbi Yaakov Kamenetzky expressed strong feelings that Mishnayos is the "*shlissel* to *Shas*" (the key to Shas). The Rosh Yeshiva recalled how Reb Chaim Soleveitchik of Brisk, famed for his deep analytical approach to Talmud study, took pride in one of his sons-in-law for having committed the entirety of Mishnayos to memory. He had found this puzzling, for it was not the type of accomplishment one associates with Brisk. Then, only a few years ago, the Rosh Yeshiva came into contact with several young men who had an unusually wide knowledge of topics from all over *Shas*. He discovered that in each case, the young men had studied Mishnayos extensively. "I then understood Reb Chaim's cause for pride," said Reb Yaakov.

Through the Rosh Yeshiva's guidance, a number of families over the past fifteen years have undertaken major Mishnayos projects for their children. A number of boys completed thirty, forty, or more *masechtos* between their 8th and 16th birthdays! These youngsters were well prepared when they began Gemara, and by the admission of their Mesivta *rebbeim*, they are considerably better in their studies than their classmates.

56.
MISHNAYOS
Part Three

n the last two chapters I discussed the importance of teaching Mishnayos. This chapter continues with some practical suggestions.

The Question

The question, then, is obvious: If experience has proven the validity of establishing a solid base of Mishnayos, why do principals and *melamdim* resist a regular Mishnah program for their students who are past the fifth or sixth grade, when they no longer "need" Mishnayos as an introduction to Torah she'b'alpeh?

Said the Rosh Yeshiva, "I'm convinced that the problem started with fathers who knew that among people who gathered in *shul* to study Torah, the *lomdim* (seasoned scholars) studied Gemara, while the less learned laymen studied Mishnayos. These fathers were impatient for their sons to become *lomdim* and prodded the *rebbe* to teach Gemara instead of dwelling on Mishnayos. The competition between *melamdim* soon forced learning Gemara earlier than advisable, in spite of the fact that according to long-standing tradition — as stated clearly in *Avos* and reiterated by authority after authority (such as the Maharal, for one) — it would have been far more beneficial to concentrate on learning additional Mishnayos rather than begin Gemara prematurely."

Suggestions for Mishnayos Study:
The Adult Possibilities

Any number of possibilities exists for adults to pursue independent study of Mishnayos. These can range from *chavrusa* (partners-in-study) programs to pocket-sized volumes for commuters.

The commentary can be as complex or self-explantory as the individual chooses. The *Mishnah Mevueres* — a comprehensive commentary written in clear Hebrew by the late Moshe Kahati, an Israeli accountant, published by Heichal Shlomo — enjoys wide popularity. Among the English language versions, Philip Blackman dominated the field for a long time, but unfortunately suffers from inaccuracies. The ArtScroll Series provides a comprehensive commentary, in addition to its clear translation of the text. Without risking overstatement, I can say that I am not alone in gaining new appreciations and insights in long-familiar Mishnayos when studying with the ArtScroll Commentary.

The Children's Program

Launching children on a Mishnayos program should be more than a trial-and-error venture, but should be carefully planned in advance. One serious misstep can effectively kill any interest in further trials. Instead, a graduated program — far safer — is recommended. Following are several practical suggestions culled from years of observation and experimentation:

(1) Set attainable goals. Obviously we would like our children to learn all 4,300 Mishnayos of *Shas*. (The author knows many youngsters who have finished one or more of the six *Sedorim* of *Shas*, and several 14-, 15-, and 16-year-olds who have finished *Shas* in its entirety, but encountering such an overwhelming goal at the start of a program is so far removed from the young child, that it can have a defeating rather than motivating effect.) The immediate goal should be the learning of one, then several *masechtos*.

(2) Start with easier *masechtos*, on subject matter within the frame of reference of the child's experience. *Masechtos* like *Berachos*, *Succah*, and selected *perakim* of *Pesachim* are especially suitable for the beginner. In fact, such Mishnayos provide an ideal *limud* (study) at the Shabbos and Yom Tov table.

57.
MISHNAYOS
Part Four

n the last chapter I offered two practical suggestions for teaching Mishnayos. I continue with four more suggestions.

After beginning with several familiar *masechtos*, switch to another area. Expand the child's horizon with *Bikkurim* (an easy *masechta*, if the preparatory groundwork is done: the first eleven *pesukim* of *Ki Savo*; skipping some of the second *perek*), *Yoma* (can you imagine the child's excitement when he is able to apply his newly gained knowledge to the study of the *avodah* section of the Yom Kippur Mussaf, and then to its recitation, once he has learned this *masechta*!), *Tamid, Eruvin, Avodah Zara, Gittin,* and so on. *Bava Kamma* and *Bava Metzia* build on familiarity with laws of damages and responsibilities picked up from *Chumash*, and also have the advantage of an excitement that relates to everyday experiences.

(3) If one or several Mishnas deal with difficult, unrelated, or sensitive subject matter, they can be skipped without disturbing continuity. Unlike Gemara, where skipping a segment tends to interrupt the train of thought, each Mishnah consists of an individual, self-contained *halachah*, and each *perek* (chapter) is a completely new subject. (In *Maseches Succah*, for example, the first *perek* deals with construction of the *succah*, the second *perek* with the mitzvah of dwelling in it, the third deals with the four species, the fourth with the four species in the *Beis HaMikdash*, and the fifth with the *Simchas Beis Hasho'eivah* and the service in the *Beis HaMikdash* on Yom Tov.) The fact that each *perek* is a separate unit is especially appealing to children with a short attention span or limited memory.

(4) Develop and sustain enthusiasm. To be sure, enthusiasm is the spark plug of any project. On a young child's level, make the completion of every *masechta*, especially the first ones, a special event. Make a *siyum* (party), and invite your son's friends and classmates (should it be less of an occasion for *simchah* than a birthday?). Present suitable gifts. Show your young son how truly proud you are of his accomplishments.

(5) The teacher should state both the immediate and long-range goals in writing. It has been demonstrated that

writing a goal is a valuable aid in crystalizing a thought, and clear thought is essential to purposeful action. The written word records where we started, determines where we are now, points to where we are heading, and spells out the approximate time-frame in which this is expected to happen.

The Pirchei Agudath Israel Mishnayos B'alpeh Contest, in which recognition is given for memorizing Mishnayos, has a major share in stimulating this new awareness of Mishnayos study. Similarly, a simple certificate distributed to students by the *rebbe* upon completion of their first *masechta* of Mishnayos encompasses the basic elements of goal-setting and recognition for effort expended.

(6) Learning Mishnayos should be an exciting, not formidable, experience. It is a serious error to introduce a new Mishnah with the foreboding words:"Concentrate, fellows, the next Mishnah is a very hard one." Mishnayos is rarely hard if the students are thoroughly prepared in advance. Even if a considerable amount of time is invested in laying the foundation for a Mishnah, so as to provide background, it is more than worthwhile if the Mishnah becomes "easy" as a result. "Now that we know the facts, learning this Mishnah is going to be really simple" might be one of the most powerful motivational tools that a parent or teacher can use, because it says to a child,"You are capable, you have the ability to understand, and I have confidence in you!"

58.

MISHNAYOS
Part Five

This is the final chapter in the Mishnayos series.

(7) Mishnayos study should be a shared objective. A young student can be taught Mishnayos by three different people, and if the objective is a considerable amount of Mishnayos, all three should be actively involved:

a. The yeshiva *rebbe*. Responding to the new awareness of Mishnayos on the part of parents and teachers, a number of yeshivos and day schools are increasing Mishnayos study in class time. The *rebbe* obviously has the educational background and methodological skills to be the prime teacher of this subject.

b. The parent. With a little preparation, thousands of yeshiva graduates can teach their children Mishnayos. For the parent who feels inadequate, the *Mishnah Mevueres* in Hebrew and the ArtScroll Series in English provide enough knowledge and confidence for teaching the young child. (Incidentally, the *Mishnah Mevueres'* introduction to Mishnayos dealing with unfamiliar subject matter can serve as a model for presenting background information to make a difficult Mishnah accessible.)

I have so often heard the claim that to adequately teach Mishnayos one must be a *talmid chacham* with a thorough knowledge of all relevent Gemaras, that I questioned Rabbi Kamenetzky in this regard. He said that given a choice between teaching Mishnayos without a broad background and not teaching at all, it is far preferable to opt for the former: Try to prepare adequately, and then teach Mishnayos, even if one is not a great *talmid chacham*.

c. The special *rebbe*. If you involve your son in a serious Mishnayos program, you may find it desirable to engage a special Mishnayos *rebbe* for him — preferably in a group with his friends. Because each Mishnah offers self-contained information that can be taught at one given session, it lends itself perfectly to special classes. Thus, on Shabbos and Sunday afternoons, one or two evenings a week, over a summer in a camp or bungalow, during Pesach and Succos vacations, a remarkable number of Mishnayos can be learned.

(8) Ideally, every new Mishnah should be repeated by the student a minimum of four times. Once, immediately after being taught, at the start of the next session, upon completion of the *perek*, and at the end of the *masechta*.

(9) Notwithstanding the success of the Pirchei Mishnayos B'alpeh Contest, learning Mishnayos by heart is not the universally suited ideal for everyone. For those who find memorization difficult, it can be a deterrent. *B'alpeh* should be encouraged for those who can handle it without difficulty, but in an either-or situation it does not pay to trade off *b'alpeh* for learning of Mishnayos altogether. Know the capabilities and limitations of the child and tailor the program accordingly. By contrast, the Pirchei's other program of completing the study of a complete *seder* by bar mitzvah is suitable for almost everyone.

There are many yeshivos who have programs of learning Mishnayos — Chemdas Program, Yeshiva Kochav Yitzchok in Baltimore; V'Dibarta Bam in numerous yeshivos — specifically not by heart, to satisfy the needs of all children.

There are few gifts that parents can bestow upon their children that are as valuable as the broadening of their horizons, motivating them to continue reaching out for bigger, better, and greater goals, and showing them how to achieve these objectives. A Mishnayos program holds out to each child just such a promise.

59.

THE SEVEN FRUSTRATIONS OF PUBLIC SPEAKING

he number seven is a major theme in a Jewish wedding. Among its appearances are the seven *berachos,* the seven times the *kallah* circles the *choson,* and the seven days of *sheva berachos.*

Recently I had the pleasure of being a guest at a lavish, catered *sheva berachos* at which there happened to be seven speakers. I was seated at a table where I could see much of the audience and gauge their interest or lack of interest in each of the speeches. I decided to listen intently to each speech, carefully watch the audience reaction, and thoughtfully discern the reason for any noticeably unpleasant or disinterested reactions.

In keeping with the theme of "seven" I would like to discuss the "seven frustrations" of a speaker's audience and offer suggestions on how a speaker can make the presentation more pleasant.

1) *Too long.* There was a time when people had the patience and *zitzfleish* (sitting power) to listen to long *derashos* and speeches. I was told of a rav who lived just 100 years ago who wrote to his students that when they speak, "they should not speak for more than an hour because people unfortunately can no longer listen to two-and three-hour speeches." In today's times, audiences generally have short attention spans, with 8 to 10 minutes the comfort zone, and 15 minutes the outside limit.

It is important that we differentiate between an "imposed" speech — such as that of a bar mitzvah — and a lecture. While speeches do have an important place at an affair or *simchah*, for the most part that is not why the guests come; rather they are there to offer congratulations, join friends, and enjoy the meal. In that sense, the speeches given there are imposed on the audience. Rare is the audience that come to a bar mitzvah to hear the speeches!

A lecture is entirely different. People go to a lecture or *shiur* primarily to hear the speaker. Either the lecturer, subject, or both are of interest to them, and they come ready to listen. When you speak well, you can safely address such an audience for 45 minutes, even an hour.

I think of a speech as "*mazon ruchani* — food for the spirit." However, too much good food is not a pleasure. Imagine a friend who has driven eight hours to attend a wedding in your city and who stops at your home to rest for a few hours. He is tired and wants to have some coffee and cake and relax. However, you prepared a five-course meal, and in an attempt to fulfill the mitzvah of *hachnasas orchim* (hospitality), you insist that he eat all five courses. He doesn't have the desire or temperament to eat your meal … but you insist! That is how I feel when a long speech is rammed down my throat at an inappropriate time or place. When a light sandwich is called for, even a gourmet steak is the wrong food!

Here is an interesting tip. If you want to speak for 5 minutes, time your speeches when you practice. If you don't do so, your actual speech will likely turn out to take 9, 10, or even 12 minutes!

Teaching yourself to speak for just a few minutes is a skill. It requires you to choose your theme carefully, to condense your main points, and to trim the fat. You may have to eliminate a point or even change the theme of your presentation to fit the time constraints.

A world–class speaker was asked how long it takes him to prepare a speech. His answer: a 10–minute speech takes two weeks' preparation. They asked him how long does it take you to prepare a one-hour speech? He answered: A one-hour speech takes a week of preparation. Finally they asked him how long does it take you to prepare a two-hour speech? He answered, "I can start now!"

60.
PUBLIC SPEAKING
Part Two

I discussed a major frustration experienced by a public speaker's audience — the imposed speech that is too long. I now continue with the next great frustration.

2. *Using words, phrases, or concepts that are not translated.* A colleague and I were in São Paulo, Brazil, where we were invited to the home of a major community activist for Shabbos. At the Friday night meal this Sephardic Jew, who did not speak any English, did his best to keep some polite conversation going in his broken Hebrew. After a little while he turned to his wife and children and began to speak in his native Portuguese. During the next few minutes, I had an

interesting sensation. I knew that my host had no intention of insulting me … yet the fact that he spoke a language that was totally foreign to me meant he was ignoring me! It was as if I were being told, "This conversation is not intended for you; it is only for learned people who understand Portuguese."

It was a put-down that was not intended, but nevertheless the sensation I had at that time was one of condescension.

We are blessed with a treasury of rich wisdom in the Torah, its many commentaries, the Talmud, and thousands of books on Jewish thought. Most often these are the sources used in a speech, and rightly so, because a Torah thought is always in place. It lends a spiritual dimension to the speech, dignifying it and giving it credence. But words of Torah can only be effective when the audience understands them. If we deliver a Torah thought in Hebrew, Aramaic, or Yiddish, and there are those in the audience who don't understand the language we use, we are not benefiting them; on the contrary, we are frustrating them. In a sense, we are setting them aside. In Yiddish there is a beautiful word to describe this feeling: *bazeitigd,* which literally means set aside, made insignificant. We must make sure to include our audience members by translating words and phrases in our speech. We also have to make sure that we convey not only the technical meaning of the word, but its "spirit" as well.

For example, we might translate "*V'Yaakov ish tam yosheiv ohalim*" simply as "Yaakov was a simple man who sat in tents," but we would do justice neither to the sentence nor to the audience. Of course, what the sentence brings immediately to the mind of a learned person is that Yaakov sat learning Torah in the *beis medrash* of Shem and the *beis medrash* of Ever. Shem and Ever were the sons of Noach who had experienced the great Flood and who knew stories about Adam HaRishon. Yaakov sat for years learning Torah from these great men … he did not merely "sit in a tent."

All of this background information is thought of in a millisecond … but only to those who know and understand it. If a speaker makes his statement and quickly translates it but does not give us the flavor of what our commentaries tell us about the statement, he cannot realistically expect his audience to understand it.

Once we know this, we can adjust our speech so that we not only translate key elements but also explain their meaning. Our presentation will now be accessible to the entire audience, and we can engage them more fully when delivering our message.

61.
PUBLIC SPEAKING
Part Three

U p to this point in our discussion of making public speaking palatable to the audience, we have mentioned the length of the speech and the need to translate expressions into English. Now on to point three.

3. *Simplify.*

The comparison of food for the body and speech for the spirit arises again and again because it is so powerful and accurate an analogy.

In preparing food for a group, we want to provide nourishment in a most enjoyable way. What we don't want to do is to prepare delicate cuisine that only a gourmet and connoisseur of food would appreciate, but that would leave the average person unfulfilled. Unless we are organizing a banquet for a very special occasion, our main objective is to prepare nourishing, filling, and enjoyable food.

Preparing a speech is similar. When a sophisticated "imposed" speech is delivered to a general audience, its intricate and hair-splitting thoughts usually go right over the heads of the majority of our listeners. If we had served such a "meal," we would have failed to meet the physical needs of our guests; as public speakers, we have failed to meet their spiritual needs.

On the other end of the spectrum is a speech that lacks any real *tochen,* content — or, as they say in Yiddish, "*shtoff.*" A Torah thought, an explanation, a provocative thought that teaches the audience a concept — these are examples of meaningful content. Even a light or humorous presentation at a *sheva berachos* should also have some *tochen.* If all we have in a speech is entertainment, we are feeding a hungry person bubble gum, which provides a burst of sweet taste but no real nourishment. Anyone who came in hungry will still be hungry afterward.

The power of speech is too valuable and the cumulative time of the audience is too important to waste by going either above or below the audience's reach.

Here is one more aspect of simplification: Don't feel obligated to say your *vort* with all the ramifications that are written in the *sefer*. You may have learned a beautiful *vort* that has one main question (and two side questions) and one main answer (augmented by three proofs).

However, just as in our example of food service, piling on very large portions when the person's capacity is limited is counterproductive. Giving your audience too much can be overwhelming for them. Instead of being able to understand and enjoy a clear answer to one clear question, the additional material only complicates the presentation. Many a listener who might have understood and enjoyed the simple version will get lost in the elaborate one, and no one benefits.

In the speaking profession, a good speaker always leaves them "asking for more."

Remember that the name of the game in good public speaking is to be *effective,* to be understood, to be remembered. By simplifying your presentation you will go a long way toward that goal.

62.
PUBLIC SPEAKING
Part Four

hroughout our series on public speaking, we have used the preparation and service of food as an analogy to the preparation and presentation of speech — food for thought.

4. *Preparation.*

Consider the following. You are a member of an important delegation who comes to visit a distant city. Many of the leading community members ask to have you as their guest, and you choose to accept the invitation of the Rubin family. You are told that supper is at 7 p.m. You arrive at 7:05 and after being cordially greeted by Mr. Rubin, you are escorted into the dining room, where you find to your amazement that the table has not been set. Mrs. Rubin comes out and says, "Thanks for coming. I'm really unprepared … but don't worry, because I'll find something in the kitchen to put together for supper."

Regardless of what happens after this point, even if the meal is enjoyable and festive, you will long remember that Mrs. Rubin essentially said, "We are unprepared for you."

The reason is simple. Respect is measured by how much preparation you do. I think about this scenario whenever I hear a speaker say, "I'm really unprepared to speak." My first reaction is, "If you, who were given weeks notice, are unprepared to speak, then I am unprepared to listen!"

I imagine a speaker uses this opening for one of two reasons: either because it sounds modest, or because he reasons that if he tells the audience he is unprepared, he has a built in excuse if he speaks poorly.

The audience does not respect either reason. They do respect a speaker who in just a few words and/or body language conveys the message, "I'm glad to be here. I have an important thought to share with you, and I have fully prepared because I respect your time and my time. So please listen to a well-constructed, concise presentation."

If you had walked into Mrs. Rubin's dining room and found a table elegantly set with china and crystal, you would have known how much they respected you and appreciated your coming to their home. During the meal, as you saw the work and effort that went into preparing each dish, you further would realize the value they have placed on having you as their guest.

I am not suggesting that the speaker necessarily tell the audience that he spent five hours preparing the speech, but he shouldn't imply that he didn't prepare.

I remember the strong comments made by a woman who was chairlady of a *mikveh* association in her town. She arranged every year to fly in a guest speaker for their annual winter *Melaveh Malkah*. Almost every speaker began by saying, "On the flight down here tonight, the following thought occurred to me … " She said to me, " I arranged for this man to speak more than four weeks ago. He is paid for the effort. Why does he prepare on the plane?"

Of course, what the speaker meant to say was that his speech was "fresh" and original — not off the shelf. But that's not what the audience heard. How much more effective it would have been if he had said, "On the plane I was reviewing my notes, and a new thought came to me." In this way, he would have let the audience know that he valued them enough to prepare in advance, and that he was still working to improve the speech even on the plane.

No person, as an individual or as member of an audience, should ever be spoken down to. We always want to make the audience feel good listening to us.

63.
PUBLIC SPEAKING
Part Five

*I*n the last chapter we discussed the importance of preparation in the creation and writing of a speech. Getting up and speaking off the cuff will seldom make for a good presentation. A speech must be well structured and well rehearsed.

In this chapter I want to suggest a method which can enhance most speeches, especially for the beginner. The method is so deceptively simple that when I first suggest it to my students in seminars, I get looks of disbelief. After you write your speech, or at least outline it, find a large empty room, lock the door, and

5. *practice delivery.* You stand up at a podium — a *shtender* will do — and recite your speech out loud.

Here are the reasons this makes for a better delivery:

1. The mechanics of reading and listening are vastly different. A sentence which may read well on paper doesn't necessarily "sound" good. Since your audience will hear your speech rather than read it, you will greatly improve the end product if you hear your own speech. This is best done in a practice run.

   When you go into your room for your private practice session, you will *hear* the words for the first time. You may find that some words which look great on paper are hard to pronounce, and you may want to change them. You will become aware of other groups of words that do not go together or that grate on your ears. As you read and recite your speech out loud, it will begin to flow more smoothly.

2. Practicing out loud gives you an opportunity to adjust your timing. Book publishers use a variety of techniques to design an inviting page. They vary typeface, margin, space between paragraphs, leave half of a page empty at the end of the chapter, and other such devices. A speaker doesn't have these printing devices available; instead he has his tone, rate of speech, and pauses between sentences as design elements which make his speech interesting and inviting.

   To be effective, these elements have to be practiced.

3. Practice enables you to go from reading your speech, which you never want to do, to delivering the speech based on key words and phrases. Each time you practice, you'll find the words come more easily. Write down your key words and phrases, and then practice glancing at this list as you speak.

   You should always have notes when you speak. Hebrew words (with punctuation), exact translations, and words which will help you remember your important points should be written on an index card in LARGE, EASY TO READ type.

4. Practice fosters self-confidence. The fear of speaking in public is well known. There is no one remedy or quick fix to get over the fear. Rather, it is chipped away little by little by building one's self-confidence.

   Granted, speaking to an empty room is not as intimidating as speaking to a live audience, but in some way this practice does help dissolve a measure of the fear.

   Two suggestions to make these practice sessions more effective: use the largest room available, and record the last — hopefully the best — of your practice sessions.

   We will develop both of these ideas in the next chapter.

64.
PUBLIC SPEAKING PRACTICE

*I*n this chapter I will discuss two techniques to help you when you speak in public. Because they are easily adaptable, they can help you in many other areas as well. We can use public speaking as a convenient model for these other applications.

I once heard an interview with a football coach who was asked the secret of his team's consistent successes.

His answer: "It's simple. We play our real game on Sunday. On Monday I give the team an extremely hard workout session. I do the same on Tuesday, Wednesday, Thursday, Friday, and Saturday. When the Sunday game finally comes ... it is the easiest game of the week!"

He made the *real* game the *easiest* game. What a beautiful, novel idea.

Make the practice sessions so tough that by comparison the real thing will be easy.

In preparation for a speech, we can use a very large, empty hall, and speak from a stage to five hundred empty chairs. Do this a number of times. When it's time for the real speech — a *sheva berachos,* for instance — with only fifty people, it will be a piece of cake!

We should teach our children (and ourselves) that while there is no glory in the preparation, you can't have the glory of the win without it.

Winning brings glory. It is often full of glamour, excitement, public acclaim, financial rewards, and deep personal satisfaction. The preparation to win involves none of these. It is lonely, hard, dull, tedious work. But you can't have the "win" without the preparation.

The lesson that to win — to do a job well — requires preparation, and that preparation is not glamorous, is a lesson that can make a world of difference in a child's future. When a youngster sees you practice two hours for a 5-minute speech, you have taught him or her an important point.

The second suggestion for creating a great presentation is to record your best practice session and ask several people to listen to it. These people should be positive, helpful, intelligent people, and you should ask them to listen with two things in mind. First, they should be alert for mistakes — mispronounced words, inaccurate quotes, thoughts not clearly presented, and the like. Second, they should offer suggestions for improving your presentation.

Give two or three friends yellow pads to write comments, and you may be amazed at what they will say.

When they give their comments, listen carefully, and openly, not defensively. If these friends are representative of your real audience and they don't understand your point, chances are your audience won't either. If you find yourself wanting to "explain" what you mean, you're on the wrong path, because your audience won't have the opportunity to ask you to explain.

We can go one step further. After you have corrected the mistakes and clarified the weak points, practice the speech again. Record it anew, and give it (and your trusty yellow pad) to a new set of friends. See if they have any criticism or comments. When you're done with this process, you'll have a vastly improved speech.

The lesson is to appreciate the importance of improvement and be willing to seek criticism. A wise man once said, "If improvement is my objective, then criticism is my ally."

This method can be used in many other areas of your life, such as writing or taking a position on a topic. Check your thinking with a few people and listen carefully to their comments. The end result will be a much better product.

65.
PUBLIC SPEAKING –
THE ROCKET SHIP

he rocket ship is an awesome invention. It stands some twenty stories high and holds hundreds of thousands of pounds of fuel, sophisticated guidance systems, tremendously powerful boosters, hundreds of computers, and miles of wires and pipes.

The irony is that this entire superstructure falls away as the rocket launch progresses.

The sole purpose of this superstructure is to place a "payload" into orbit. The payload could be a relatively small package, a basketball–sized communication system.

A child may ask, "Why do they need to build the expensive superstructure just to get the payload up there? Why don't they just throw the payload up into space?" Obviously the answer is that to place a payload exactly where you want it, you can't just throw it; you have to position it carefully.

Can you imagine how foolish the rocket scientists would be if they built this gigantic superstructure but failed to place the payload on the rocket?

A speech is similar to the rocket in the sense that it has a superstructure and payload. The superstructure is composed of several possible elements: the opening, the story, the joke, the anecdote, the *Chazal,* and everything else that is designed to convey the payload.

The payload is the message, the kernel, the basic reason we make this particular speech to this particular audience. Only when the message is clearly defined can it become a meaningful payload. When the speaker doesn't have the "payload" clear in his own mind, there is little chance of conveying it to the audience.

I once took a course in writing direct mail. The instructor insisted that at the top of every letter we state in one sentence exactly what we want the letter to do. For example, if we were to write a sales letter for a chair manufacturer, we had to write on top of the page, "I want to sell assembly-style plastic stackable chairs for $20 each."

When we questioned the need for this, he explained that a writer often gets carried away by his own words and gets lost. He forgets the purpose of his letter. By writing the one sentence on the top of the page, he constantly reminds himself of his purpose and stays on target.

This applies to a speech as well, even more so! Often a speaker falls in love with his thoughts and gets carried away. One beautiful story leads to a new thought, which leads to another story. All well and good, all very enjoyable. But what is the message — where is the "payload" that he wants the audience to carry home?

Imagine that you gave a very good speech. One of the people in the audience then goes home and tells his spouse about the great speech. The wife asks him to tell her what the speaker said.

At this moment you want your audience member to repeat the "payload"... the essence, the main idea. If he were to repeat the story or joke you told, but miss the payload, you would be disappointed. If he tells his wife the major point you made, your superstructure was right on target.

We suggest that you write the one or two main sentences, the payload of your speech, and keep it in front of you as you write and practice your speech. The audience can't hear the message any more clearly than the speaker delivers it. It is in the speaker's best interest to keep the message clear to himself at all times.

66.
A DRIVE IN THE RANCH

magine that a good friend has invited you to join him for a few days on his 2,000-acre Texas ranch. As a way of entertaining you, he offers you his Jeep and a picnic lunch, and says, "Take my Jeep, drive wherever you want, and enjoy yourself. Since I own all the property for miles, you can go wherever you care to go."

You go out and follow a dirt road that leads to a path. Then you drive across grassy fields and alongside shallow streams. There are no fences, no set boundaries, just open fields. You have a ball.

Next year you visit your friend again, and once again he offers you his Jeep. But this time he cautions you that he has built various fences on his property. There is now a fence along the dirt road, another fence near a field, and one along the stream. While there are still plenty of open spaces to drive through, you can no longer go wherever you want!

The *Meiri* gives us a beautiful new meaning to a familiar Mishnah in *Pirkei Avos*. The Mishnah says, "Make a fence to (protect) the Torah." The usual explanation is that we are being taught to protect a commandment of the Torah by creating a "fence" around it. Not writing on Shabbos is a Torah commandment. Not touching a pencil on Shabbos is a rabbinical commandment, or fence, protecting a person from violating the Torah.

The *Meiri* says that this Mishnah comes to teach us that when a person speaks in public, especially to deliver *divrei Torah* (Torah teachings), he should not make it difficult for the audience to absorb. Rather, he should speak only "at the appropriate time, the appropriate amount, in the appropriate place, and about the appropriate subject." We are being taught that even in teaching Torah, the speaker is obligated to choose the appropriate time, amount of material, place, and subject.

This *Meiri* teaches us that a speaker or teacher should *not* think that the audience is "obligated" to learn just because he is teaching Torah. He cannot, therefore, deliver his presentation any way he wants to, and let the listener figure it out.

It is clearly the speaker's responsibility to prepare and make the speech interesting, enjoyable, and easy to listen to. It is also the teacher's obligation to make the lesson interesting, enjoyable, and easy to listen to.

Just as the fences on the Texas ranch provide guidelines, so too the four "fences" of public speaking — appropriate time, amount, place, and subject — provide guidance to the speaker.

When we speak to an audience, when we teach a group, we are asking our audience to allow us access to their minds. We are saying, "Please think along with me." We are asking them to share their most important possession — their minds. That is not a request to be taken lightly. If we want the audience to oblige, we have to do our share.

Public speaking is not a "free-for-all"; it's a sacred trust.

67.
CAPTIVE AUDIENCE

ave you ever heard the phrase "a captive audience"? It is usually used to refer to an audience that has to listen to the speaker because it has no easy or polite way to "escape" — thus the word "captive."

Three examples of a captive audience are a congregation in *shul*, the guests at a *sheva berachos,* and a first grade class.

In the example of the *shul*, the rabbi often speaks before the reading of the Torah. We can reason that since it is impolite for congregants to walk out before or in the midst of the rabbi's sermon, they are "captive" and the rabbi can say what he wants because the audience has to listen.

The same principle applies to a *sheva berachos* meal. The thinking is that since we ate our host's chicken, we owe it to him to listen to the speeches. Whether we want to or not, common courtesy demands that we sit at the table. Thus the speaker has a locked-in audience.

The third example, that of a first grade class, is the easiest to imagine. The small children can't even get out of their seats without the teacher's permission, so in a sense they really are captives.

When a speaker has a captive audience, he is assured that they are listening. Right?

Wrong!

The audience may be sitting in front of you; they may even be looking directly at you. But in their minds they can instantly turn you off. The fact that the people who are sitting before you can't politely walk out in no way reduces your obligation to prepare well and speak well. It is the prime challenge of the speaker to develop and maintain the audience's interest.

Last chapter we wrote of a *Meiri* that taught us that a speaker has to be sensitive to the appropriate time, amount, place, and subject of his speech. There is another *Meiri* that takes this point even further. In his commentary to *Mishlei* he writes that a speaker has to present his material so that it will be as sweet to the audience as "milk and honey mixed together." Then he adds, "If anyone teaches

Torah publicly and does not present it sweetly, better it *not be said!"*

(I don't pretend to understand the *Meiri's* statement that Torah which is not presented sweetly should not be said, but perhaps the reason may be that people who hear Torah presented "not sweetly" may get turned off.)

We now have a relatively easy-to-use yardstick with which to evaluate our presentation. We can ask ourselves, "Will this type of an opening, whether it is a *Chazal,* story, example, joke, or argument, interest my audience or not?"

I once suggested to a rabbi that he record his speech when he was practicing it and listen critically to find ways to improve it. A few days later he informed me that my idea didn't work. He explained that he had recorded it and tried to listen to it … and then sheepishly admitted that he had fallen asleep listening to his own speech! I had very little to say after that.

Bring yourself to listen objectively, for there is no better way to evaluate your speech. When you adopt quality of interest as your gold standard, you will have taken a quantum leap toward becoming a highly effective public speaker.

68.
TEACHING CHILDREN TO SPEAK IN PUBLIC
Part One

*S*peaking clearly, concisely, and effectively is one of the most desirable skills that we can teach children. Effective public speaking will enable the child to feel comfortable in communicating his ideas to individuals or to a group, a skill he will carry with him into adulthood.

How important is this skill to a child's future? In addition to helping him build clarity of thought, self-expression, and leadership ability, public speaking is a tremendous aid in developing self-esteem. Standing in front of an audience, presenting one's thoughts in an orderly and interesting manner, and winning the approval of a group is a powerful reinforcement of personal self-worth, which can become the motivation for many other activities.

How does one teach children to speak in public?

There are two simple, but not necessarily easy, pieces of advice.

1. Don't make a big deal over it.

2. Don't criticize.

The first point, not making a fuss over it, is meant to ignore or chip away at the fear many of us have about public speaking. If we announce to the family or to the class that every child will be giving a "public speech," and insist the child stand at a podium, we can easily create the adult fears and inhibitions that many children don't have — but can quickly acquire.

Let's begin by asking a child to say a *dvar Torah* on the *parshah*. At home, you can ask the child to speak from his or her seat, and in a very informal way. If you're going to have company at the table, offer to practice the *dvar Torah* beforehand so that the child will not be embarrassed. If there is resistance, don't insist until the child feels comfortable speaking in front of guests.

I have seen this work both in the home and in the classroom. In the class, if a *rebbe* or *morah* can have a student say a short, two-minute *vort* every second or third week, almost every student will acquire the ability to speak comfortably in public. I know this to be a fact, because I often ask good speakers how they learned to project so well. Invariably they answer, "My grade-school teacher had us speak almost every week."

Public speaking should be broached naturally, matter-of-factly. Don't turn it into a big deal. Assume every child can and will do it. Offer your assistance when necessary, and give much praise.

Once the child has spoken tens of times from his seat, ask him to stand when he says the *dvar Torah*. The next step would be to intoduce a lectern or *shtender* and follow that by moving the lectern ten feet away from the table. If you take each step slowly — almost as a game — allowing the child to become comfortable with it before advancing to the next stage, you will have the child speaking in public as a matter-of-fact in a natural way... the way it should be.

Second, don't criticize. This may be a simple concept, but for the parents or teachers who strive for perfection in a child or student, this may be the most difficult challenge. In fact, refraining from criticism might very well be the single most important rule to follow in many areas of education, and of life. We will devote the next chapter to it.

69.
TEACHING CHILDREN TO SPEAK IN PUBLIC
Part Two

*T*he previous chapter introduced the benefits of teaching children to speak in public. It emphasized the importance of refraining from criticism in the process.

One of the major difficulties in learning to speak in public is that you are putting your ego on the line. Every time you speak, you expose your thoughts to a roomful of people, each of whom can put you down in many ways. Every member of the audience is capable of overtly (and covertly) laughing at something you said, the way you said it, or something you did while standing at the lectern. Whether or not anyone actually does laugh is irrelevant. Just the possibility is enough to make public speaking something most people go to great lengths to avoid.

Criticism can cut through to a child's core and torpedo his self-confidence. Your suggestions may improve the presentation by 2 percent, but you risk destroying his self-confidence by 50 percent!

More than twenty years ago I was asked by Torah Umesorah to give a course in public speaking to *kollel* men. In researching the subject, I learned that a high percentage of graduates of public speaking courses given by universities hate to speak in public. They may know the mechanics of how to prepare and deliver a speech but they have a genuine distaste for the whole process. I wanted to learn the reason, and asked many people this question.

Finally it dawned on me that the way this subject is taught produces a large measure of anxiety. After teaching the fundamentals of public speaking, the professor typically assigns a student to speak in class. As the student speaks the instructor sits in the back and takes notes. As soon as the student finishes his speech, the instructor immediately informs him of all the mistakes he just made. In most cases the student is humiliated. Speaking in public is challenging enough to most students, but being dressed down in public — even by a well-meaning professor — is more than most people can handle. As a result, they are so hurt that they decide never to speak in public again if they can help it. Public speaking to them means public embarrassment.

Once I fully understood the problem, I decided to introduce a public-speaking course with the reassurance that neither I nor anyone else in the class would criticize the speaker. Once the students believed and trusted me, once they saw that it really happened — that they spoke and I did not criticize them — there was a release of tension, and the doorway to learning was thrown wide open. Students learn by observing how others speak and by listening to general suggestions for improvement. (When there is no other way, I offer a suggestion in private.)

It has been said that sometimes the greatest use of one's mouth in helping a child or student is to bite one's tongue.

That statement is probably true in many areas of helping children grow. It is especially true in teaching public speaking.

The Pocket Scroll® Series